Understanding
Pensions

Robert Gaines

Croner
a Wolters Kluwer business

Wolters Kluwer (UK) Limited
145 London Road
Kingston upon Thames
Surrey KT2 6SR
Tel: 020 8247 1175

Published by
Wolters Kluwer (UK) Limited
145 London Road
Kingston upon Thames
Surrey KT2 6SR
Tel: 020 8247 1175

First published March 2011
Second Edition 2012

ISBN 978–1–85524–764–2

Printed in the UK by Hobbs the Printers Ltd, Totton, Hampshire.

PREFACE

Pensions could be characterised as one of the defining topics of our times. They are a subject of daily discussion at our place of work, leisure or through the media. This may reflect the words of the song "you don't know what you've got 'til its gone" and the last 20 years have disturbed that cosy security that many employees and employers felt about their pension scheme.

Yet few people understand pensions, fewer still understand what their rights and entitlements are and even fewer prepare adequately for their retirement.

Pensions are not easy. The subject is dry and full of jargon, but the rewards are valuable.

This book covers the main areas of pensions with the intention of demystifying them. It aims to help readers focus on what matters to them and to remove anxieties which knowledge demonstrates may be unjustified.

It discusses some subjects in the context of today's economic and business environment and addresses common themes that can be a feature of a wide variety of schemes. It identifies much of the jargon and gives a simple description. It explains rights and entitlements, for example in the event of corporate failure. Indeed it replies directly to the question "how safe is my pension?" This is a classic example of a short question with a long answer.

There are also sections on trustee responsibilities (in particular investment): the Pensions Regulator expects trustees to maintain an understanding of their job. Employers will want to understand the choices that lie before them, especially with the imminent implementation of automatic enrolment.

Much of the regulation of pensions can be categorised as "tax" (meaning the supervision of very generous tax reliefs afforded to pension schemes) and member protection and those topics feature prominently.

Yet no consideration would be properly complete for the individual without a section on the State scheme and contracting-out so that is also covered.

Pension schemes are part of our remuneration. It is as important (if not more so) to understand what they can do for us.

This is the second edition of this book. It has been updated to reflect changes to the tax rules in the Finance Act 2011, the Pensions Act 2011, including the auto-enrolment scheme, which received the Royal Assent after some last-minute changes in October 2011 and the announcements made at the time of the Autumn Statement in November 2011.

April 2012

AUTHOR

Robert Gaines

Robert Gaines has worked with pensions for 30 years. During most of that time he has held senior positions in life assurance companies, but for the last 10 years he has been self-employed, sharing his time between training, consulting and writing.

He is the author of *The Pensions Factbook* that was published in 1988 and continues to be updated. Since 1988 he has contributed to many other publications, including a number for Wolters Kluwer.

Contents

CHAPTER 1

Introduction

Trends

Pension schemes come in many shapes and sizes, but the objective is the same for all: to enable individuals and employers to put money aside for retirement. They may be funded by an individual who is self-employed or employed, or they may be funded by an employer or group of employers. When they are funded by an employer, membership of the pension scheme is regarded as an important element of the remuneration package and the pension benefit is sometimes described as "deferred pay".

Pension schemes are recognised as a good thing, but it has become increasingly difficult to persuade individuals to save, especially over the long term. This trend has been accompanied by a reduction in the quality and amount of employer provision at the same time as the cost of providing a lifetime income has increased. As a very rough guide, for every five years of working life, we can look forward to two years of retirement.

The challenge was recognised as early as the start of the 20th century (although pension schemes have been around for longer) when the law recognised that employers should be allowed to treat contributions to a pension scheme as a necessary expense of business and, therefore, not subject to tax. This was followed by a move to more extensive tax reliefs for contributions and funds in order to incentivise employers, employees and the self-employed to save for retirement.

Tax reliefs are only part of the solution and inappropriate for the many who simply have insufficient disposable income or capital to save. The tax incentives are complemented therefore, by a contributory State pension scheme and a means-tested State pension credit benefit.

More recently, as the cost of State benefits in an era of low taxes has started to cause concern, governments have reduced State benefits and legislated for low-cost private pensions.

The Choice for the Private Sector Employer

The private sector employer has a wide range of choices when determining what type of pension scheme to provide for employees. Today, the motivation will only be paternalistic if that suits a commercial objective and the first choice will be between pension benefits and other employee benefits or cash or a combination of these.

The likely motivators will include legal obligations, tax, cost and the importance of recruitment and retention of employees.

Types of Scheme

Occupational or personal pension scheme?

Historically, an occupational scheme was established by an employer and employees were invited to join. The employer determined the rules and benefit structure of the scheme which was then administered on behalf of trustees by a scheme administrator. Trusts are a particularly English concept and have never satisfactorily been described. Put simply, they enable the legal ownership of assets to be separated from the beneficial entitlement (meaning the right to derive an income or other financial benefit in this context).

So the "ownership" of assets as most people would recognise it is in the name of the trustees, as a means of giving effect to the rights belonging to the members.

The primary financial obligation of the trustees is to the members and the assets are held by the trustees to give effect to the members' pension entitlements and rights.

Personal pension schemes are operated by a variety of organisations including life assurance companies and smaller firms. The relationship between the operator and the member is often contractual rather than fiduciary (deriving from a trust).

The firm establishes a scheme and individuals are invited to join the scheme. The individuals become members on joining and are allocated arrangements that are evidenced by a policy or plan. The important feature of personal pension schemes for these purposes is that they are not established by the employer and the rules are not determined by the employer, but an employer may decide to make membership available (and may offer a facility to collect and pay contributions to a designated scheme).

Perhaps the main difference between these two types of scheme is that occupational schemes (also known as retirement benefit schemes) can offer defined benefits (see below), whereas this is impractical under a personal pension scheme.

Statutory definition of an occupational scheme
"Occupational pension scheme" means a pension scheme:
(a) that:
    (i) for the purpose of providing benefits to, or in respect of, people with service in employments of a description, or
    (ii) for that purpose and also for the purpose of providing benefits to, or in respect of, other people, is established by, or by persons who include, a person to whom subsection (2) [employers — author's note] applies, and
(b) that has its main administration in the United Kingdom or outside the Member States, or a pension scheme that is prescribed or is of a prescribed description.
"Personal pension scheme" means a pension scheme that:
(a) is not an occupational pension scheme, and
(b) is established by a person within any of the paragraphs of s.154(1) of the **Finance Act 2004** (*essentially authorised under the Financial Services and Markets Act 2000 — author's note*).

Activities of occupational pension schemes
1. If an occupational pension scheme has its main administration in the United Kingdom, the trustees or managers of the scheme must secure that the activities of the scheme are limited to retirement-benefit activities.
2. Subsection (1) does not apply to a scheme if it is a prescribed scheme or a scheme of a prescribed description.
3. Section 10 of the **Pensions Act 1995** (civil penalties) applies to a trustee or manager of a scheme to which subsection (1) applies if:

    (a) the scheme has activities that are not retirement-benefit activities, and

    (b) the trustee or manager has failed to take all reasonable steps to secure that the activities of the scheme are limited to retirement-benefit activities.

4. In this section "retirement-benefit activities" means:

    (a) operations related to retirement benefits, and

    (b) activities arising from operations related to retirement benefits.

5. In subsection (4) "retirement benefits" means:

    (a) benefits paid by reference to reaching, or expecting to reach, retirement, and

    (b) benefits that are supplementary to benefits within paragraph (a) and that are provided on an ancillary basis:

        (i) in the form of payments on death, disability or termination of employment, or

        (ii) in the form of support payments or services in the case of sickness, poverty or need, or death.

A consequence of this definition is that employees who are only eligible for a grouped personal pension scheme may not join the occupational scheme on a "life cover only" basis.

The Structure of Retirement Benefits

Defined benefit, money purchase or cash balance

Fifty years ago, occupational schemes were synonymous with defined benefits, but attitudes and business imperatives have changed. There are many variations of the design but, put simply, a defined benefit scheme promises a pension (part of which can usually be commuted to a lump sum) calculated by reference to "final salary" or an average lifetime salary, years of pensionable service and an accrual rate. The accrual rate will typically be expressed as a fraction ($\frac{1}{60}$th, $\frac{1}{80}$th, 1.25%) for each year of pensionable service.

The member has no proprietary interest in the assets of the scheme, but has rights that are delivered by the trustees. The rights are defined in the scheme trust deed, rules and the general law.

4

Employers regard the main disadvantage of a defined benefit scheme as being the cost and its unpredictable nature. It is impossible to predetermine the input and the output from an investment, and because the output (the benefit) is determined by the scheme rules, the contribution must adjust from time to time to ensure that the pension fund is adequate to meet its financial objective.

Very often a funding shortfall is caused by factors beyond the control of the employer such as a fall in investment yields or an increase in the cost of providing a lifetime income if only because individuals are living longer meaning that under each scheme there are more people at older ages claiming a retirement pension. It is sometimes said that the investment risk under a defined benefit scheme falls on the sponsor (employer).

The funding cost has been supplemented in recent years by two additional factors.

1. The increasing cost of complying with rules designed to protect members' rights before retirement.
2. The increasing cost of funding the compensation scheme (Pension Protection Fund).

On the face of it, the member will be attracted by the prospect of a pension that is linked to pay and indeed this type of scheme has been referred to as the "Rolls Royce" of pension schemes in the past. Some commentators have injudiciously described benefits as "guaranteed". Now older and wiser, we appreciate that the benefit is only as strong as the employer's promise and the employer's ability to keep the scheme adequately funded (see below). The promise is sometimes called the employer "covenant".

Few employers wish to offer defined benefit schemes nowadays and the preference is for money purchase or defined contribution schemes. Under a defined contribution scheme, each member is allocated a policy or account to which the employer and/or the member pays a predetermined contribution such as 7% of pay. There is no predetermined benefit as under a defined benefit scheme. The pension (and lump sum) will be determined by the performance of the investments (net of charges) until benefits are taken, the term over which they are invested and the rate at which the investment is converted to income, usually in the form of an annuity (itself dependent on prevailing interest rates and life expectancy).

So as a general rule, under a money purchase scheme, it is said that the investment risk is borne by the member. The administration costs of

5

the scheme may be expressed as a percentage of the fund, but the employer may pay these fees separately and restrict the fund to investment management fees.

Cash balance schemes are relatively rare. The principle is that the employer awards pension rights during employment and these are recorded by the scheme (and revalued) until they can be converted to retirement benefits at pension age. The benefits are not entirely calculated by reference to contributions paid from year to year. They are essentially money purchase schemes although the employer is responsible for meeting the cost of revaluation. The risk is primarily taken by the member.

Some schemes combine more than one of these designs and they are called "hybrid" schemes. For example, a scheme may provide a predetermined income supplemented by a money purchase (open-ended) benefit.

Public Sector (Public Service Schemes)

These are schemes for individuals who are employed in the public sector such as employees of the NHS and local government, firefighters, police and civil servants. They are defined benefit schemes and are generally unfunded (the notable exception being the local government scheme which is funded by the local authorities).

Unfunded public sector schemes do not hold assets and are not subject to a trust. They pay benefits from current revenues which derive from taxation. So, for example, Parliament determines from time to time and on the advice of the Government Actuary what should be the contribution to support the provision of benefits to pensioner members and beneficiaries of the Police Pension Scheme (and the New Police Pension Scheme).

An unfunded scheme contribution is primarily sensitive to the ratio of contributors to claimants which is itself sensitive to historic birth rates and life expectancy.

Contributory or Non-contributory

The contribution here is the member's contribution. The employer may require the member to contribute to the scheme as a condition of membership. The member may "volunteer" to pay contributions (AVCs) above this requirement to increase benefits if the scheme allows it.

It is unusual for the employer to change the rate of personal contribution. Defined benefit schemes are sometimes called "balance of cost" schemes and this refers to the employer's "obligation" to contribute whatever is necessary above the member contribution to ensure that the scheme is adequately funded. So, if the required contribution is 12% and the member contribution is 4%, the balance of cost is a contribution of 8%.

It may be that a defined benefit scheme is in surplus and, in those circumstances, the employer will usually suspend or reduce its contribution, but continue to require the member contribution.

Nowadays, most, if not all, defined benefit schemes have serious funding shortfalls at the same time as trading conditions are difficult. Furthermore, (and as we shall see) the funding status of the scheme must now be reflected in the sponsoring company's accounts. Employers are therefore taking drastic action to manage their liabilities. They can do this in two ways:

1. They can restrict benefits and/or membership. The problem is that existing entitlement is protected so any change takes time to work through.
2. They can increase employer and/or member contributions.

The employer may require the member to contribute as a condition of membership of a money purchase scheme, but because the benefit is not predetermined there is less need to change the rate once it has been set.

Registration and Tax Reliefs

It has long been public policy to allow tax privileges to pension schemes. The thrust of the tax legislation is to defer liability to income tax on earned income so that employers and individuals will put money aside for retirement and minimise the claim on State benefits and care. The tax rules were substantially simplified for most people with effect from 6 April 2006 ("A" day) although they remain challenging for some special classes.

The way the tax reliefs work can be summarised as follows.

• In order to claim reliefs from taxes that would normally apply to capital gains and income derived from assets, the scheme must be registered with HM Revenue and Customs (HMRC). Permission is not required, but registration can be withdrawn if, for example, information is misrepresented to HMRC or tax not paid.

- Registration allows a wide range of reliefs within certain allowances. There are few limits: if an allowance is exceeded, HMRC simply applies a tax charge on the excess. If the scheme makes an unauthorised payment (such as exceeding the lump sum allowance or investing in "taxable property") HMRC will apply tax charges. The allowances against income and corporation taxes refer to "input" and "output".

The impact of accumulated tax reliefs is substantial, but some of those reliefs will be recovered when the pension is paid (pension schemes remain tax efficient if only because a large proportion of the benefit is payable as a tax-free lump sum). For many people, income will fall in retirement, as will their marginal tax rate and the proportion represented by the personal allowance increases.

This method of encouraging savers differs from most foreign systems and indeed the Individual Savings Account (ISA) where there is no tax relief on input, but output is tax-free.

The tax reliefs available to registered pension schemes are:

(a) employer contributions are a tax deductible business expense for the employer
(b) employer contributions within allowances are not taxed on the member
(c) member contributions within allowances are relievable against the member's highest marginal rate of income tax
(d) funds are not generally subject to UK tax on income and capital gains; they are unable to reclaim the tax credit on dividends and neither are they exempt from stamp duty or VAT
(e) part of the retirement benefit is available as a tax-free lump sum
(f) any lump sum paid on death before retirement benefits are taken is usually free of inheritance tax.

Types of Member

At any one time, an occupational scheme will include different classes of member.

Active members are individuals who continue to accrue benefits under the scheme or for whom contributions continue to be paid.

Pensioner members are those members who have started to claim benefits.

Dependants are those individuals who are being paid a pension based on a deceased person's accrual. Typically, they could be a widow, widower, ex-civil partner or another individual who was financially dependent.

Deferred members are those individuals who have accrued benefits in the scheme, but no longer do so. Neither are they yet drawing benefits. *Pension credit members* are individuals who have not accrued benefits in respect of their own employment, but have been awarded a pension credit as part of a divorce settlement.

Early Leavers

It is common for a member to cease being an active member before taking retirement benefits. This is usually because he or she leaves the job to which the pension is related. Under a money purchase scheme, the fund continues to go up or down in value to reflect the underlying investment performance. It can then be applied to providing benefits by, for example, annuity purchase at pension age.

Before pension age, the fund may be transferred to any other registered pension scheme (if it were not registered, the transfer would be unauthorised and heavily taxed).

Under a defined benefit scheme there is a set of "preservation" rules that protect the rights of the early leaver who does not have an identifiable "pot" of money such as is available under a money purchase scheme.

The preservation rules apply when pension rights are said to have vested after completing two years' active service in the scheme. The scheme rules may specify a shorter vesting period and money purchase schemes will usually offer "immediate" vesting on joining the scheme.

If there is a vesting period and the member leaves within the vesting period, the member now has two options:
- they may take a refund of personal contributions less tax in which case any benefit accrual is extinguished, or
- if they have completed three months' service, they can transfer the value of the accrued benefit to another scheme such as a personal pension scheme (unlike the refund of personal contributions, the transfer value includes employer contributions).

The preservation rules require that benefits for an early leaver whose benefits have vested after two years' service must be calculated on the same basis as for a member who takes benefits at retirement age. As a matter of practice, the three-month value will be calculated on the same basis.

> **Example**
> The XYZ pension scheme offers a pension from normal retirement date of ⅟₆₀th of final salary for each year of service. Jo leaves service at the age of 40 after completing 10 years' service. The preserved pension will usually be ¹⁰⁄₆₀ths of final salary at date of leaving.

The preservation rules also include revaluation requirements in order to protect the real value of preserved pensions against price inflation. The main measure is known as "limited price indexation". Limited Price Indexation (LPI) has generally referred to an increase by the lesser of 2.5% a year (originally 5%) and the "general increase in prices". Until 2011 this was taken to mean the increase in the Retail Prices Index (RPI) although some schemes drafted their rules widely enough to accommodate other measures if the law so allowed. From April 2011, schemes may use the RPI or the Consumer Prices Index (CPI) if their rules permit it. The CPI excludes the main housing costs and tends to increase at a slower rate than the RPI. Schemes that refer to the RPI in their rules will not be subject to a statutory override and the Government has no intention of relaxing the rules that make it practically impossible to modify benefits that have already accrued.

If the preserved pension includes guaranteed minimum pension (GMP) in respect of contracted-out service prior to 1997, the GMP will revalue in line with earnings in order to retain its link with the earnings-related State pension. As an alternative, the scheme may revalue the GMP at a fixed rate that is determined by the date of leaving service. For the period 2007–2012, the rate is set at 4% a year and from 2012–2017, it will be 4.75% a year.

The preservation rules also influence the calculation of transfer values. We will look at these in more detail later, but the transfer value (known as a "cash equivalent transfer value" if benefits have vested after two years' service) must derive from the preserved pension and the same assumptions as are used in valuing the scheme as a whole (eg rates of investment return, interest rate). The transfer value must be a fair representation of the accrued pension.

How to Calculate a Transfer Value

1. Identify the accrued pension.
2. Revalue the pension to normal retirement date under the scheme.
3. Determine the value of fund required to provide the pension (based on interest rates/gilt yields).

4. Apply a discount rate (assumed rate of return) to the fund above in order to identify its present value (the transfer value).

This calculation is very sensitive to assumptions made about discount rates, interest rates, etc. The assumptions are determined from time to time by the trustees on the advice of their actuary.

Retirement Age

The employer will be influenced by two sets of rules in determining the retirement age under the scheme: age equality legislation and HMRC rules.

The age equality legislation requires pensions to be available on the same terms at the same age for men and women and some other groups. HMRC rules generally require benefits to be taken no earlier than 55 ("normal minimum pension age") in order to be treated as authorised payments.

Various terms are used to describe pension age and each may have a distinct meaning.

For example:

normal retirement date or age (NRD or NRA) — this date appears in the scheme rules and is used primarily as a "target" to determine the cost of funding a defined benefit scheme

normal pension age — the earliest date at which the member can take benefits without permission of the trustees and without an actuarial reduction. It is normally the same as normal retirement date and is rarely used

selected pension age — the date the member actually chooses to take benefits.

Under a defined benefit scheme it is usual for the benefit to be subject to an actuarial reduction if benefits are taken before the normal pension age (normal retirement date). This is to reflect the fact that the pension is payable for longer and will therefore cost more: the impact could otherwise be detrimental to other members. Very often, the employer will negotiate a special contribution with the trustees to "make up" the actuarial reduction for a senior employee or if an employee is being made redundant.

Ill-health Retirement ("Involuntary Retirement")

There will be circumstances when an individual is prevented from working to a normal pension age because of an illness or accident. In normal circumstances, if benefits are taken before normal minimum pension age (eg 55) they will be taxed heavily as unauthorised payments.

If the member is unable to carry on his or her normal job because of illness or injury, the retirement benefit may be crystallised regardless of age without the benefit being taxed as unauthorised. It will be taxed as a retirement benefit (tax-free lump sum and taxed income).

If the member subsequently recovers and is able to return to work then the pension may be suspended (or partially suspended) although if the pension is a scheme pension, the opinion of a medical practitioner will again be required.

If a registered medical practitioner is of the opinion that life expectancy is less than 12 months, the value of benefits may be paid as a tax-free lump sum at any age. It will then fall into the estate so the member, relatives and advisors may wish to consider that on death in service before age 75, a lump sum may be paid tax-free and will by-pass the estate. If the member claims the serious ill-health lump sum after the 75th birthday, the lump sum will be taxed at 55% (and may then form part of the estate). This consideration is only of real relevance under a money purchase scheme which would use a return of fund to provide much of the death benefit (unlike a defined benefit scheme).

Contracting-out

As we shall see, the State pension scheme comprises a flat-rate (basic) State pension (for employees and the self-employed) and an additional, earnings-related pension for employees. The earnings-related pension has variously been called a graduated pension, the State earnings-related pension (SERPS) and the State second pension (S2P).

The State scheme is contributory and not means-tested.

The employer's option to contract out allows the employer and employees to pay lower National Insurance contributions in return for employees giving up entitlement to the additional State pension and the employer providing a benefit under a private arrangement.

A similar option was available to individual employees, but is withdrawn from April 2012.

Certain formalities and requirements accompany the option to contract-out and these have changed over the years. Between 1978 and 1997, the occupational scheme had to undertake to provide a guaranteed minimum pension under a defined benefit scheme and this was roughly equal to the SERPS foregone.

From 1997, defined benefit schemes simply had to mirror or exceed the benefits of a "model scheme".

Money purchase schemes were able to contract out from 1988. Contracting-out on a money purchase basis was abolished from April 2012 and accrued benefits will be treated as any other benefits.

Inflation-proofing

Pensions from defined benefit schemes must offer a limited measure of inflation-proofing. A number of public service schemes (most notably the Civil Service Pension Scheme) had originally linked pensions in payment to the increases in the Retail Prices Index (RPI). From 2011, public sector schemes will replace the RPI measure with a measure against the Consumer Prices Index (CPI). The CPI generally increases at a lower rate than the RPI and both are considered to underperform pensioner inflation.

In the 1980s, the concept of limited price indexation was introduced as a requirement for preserved pensions from defined benefit schemes in the private sector. So, if an individual left service with a preserved pension, its value would be substantially maintained against inflation until it was taken.

The limited price indexation (LPI) requirement was originally to increase the preserved pension (excluding contracted-out rights) by the lesser of the increase in the RPI and 5%. The principle was extended to pensions in payment from 1997 and since then, the 5% "cap" on the requirement has become 2.5% for preserved pensions and pensions in payment.

From 2011, the inflation index, for these purposes may either be the RPI or the Consumer Prices Index (CPI), but only if the scheme rules allow it. This change extends to the inflation measure for public service schemes.

Inflation-proofing demonstrates the dilemma for lawmakers. It may seem attractive to require pensions to increase with inflation without cap, but the cost (and the reserved cost) would probably deter employers from providing the benefit in the first place. The requirements of a defined benefit scheme always balance the interests of members against those of the employer in a relatively free market.

Some commentators have advocated risk-sharing under which inflation protection might be suspended for a period in which the scheme was in deficit. This option is not available under current legislation and there seems no appetite on the part of government to introduce it.

The Choice for the Employee

Although the attempt to simplify pensions from April 2006 has often been derided, the rules took some giant steps towards simplification for the majority of employees. Barriers to personal saving in one type of scheme if the employee was contributing to another were swept away and the rules were built on simple allowances relating to aggregate input and aggregate output.

The main choices made available to the employee may therefore be:

- if the employer provides no pension scheme, whether to contribute to a personal pension plan
- if the employer provides membership of an occupational pension scheme, group personal pension scheme or stakeholder scheme (or the National Employment Savings Trust (NEST)), whether to join or opt out of the employer scheme
- if the employer provides membership of a scheme, whether to top-up those savings with contributions to a personal pension scheme, stakeholder scheme or NEST.

The Choice for the Self-employed

The choice for the self-employed is similar to that available to employees (deliberately). However, it is rare for the self-employed to be offered membership of an occupational pension scheme although recent legislation allows for the possibility in respect of contractors.

Key Facts

- Pension provision in the UK derives from a State pension, tax privileged private arrangements and means-tested benefits.
- An employer may offer an occupational pension scheme or access to a personal pension scheme.
- Occupational schemes are established under a trust by the employer and this separates the employer from the members' interests under the scheme.
- The three main benefit structures are defined benefit, defined contribution and cash balance.
- Under a defined benefit scheme the contribution is unpredictable and these schemes are reducing in number in favour of defined contribution schemes under which the benefit is unpredictable.
- A defined benefit scheme may be underfunded for a variety of reasons including poor investment performance and improved mortality.
- Public sector schemes are usually defined benefit schemes and usually unfunded.
- Schemes may require a contribution from the member. Employers are required to ensure that defined benefit schemes are properly funded and this gives rise to the description of these schemes as "balance of cost" schemes.
- A pension scheme qualifies for a range of tax reliefs if it is registered. Tax will be charged if allowances are exceeded or unauthorised payments made from the scheme.
- If a member leaves a scheme after two years, but before taking retirement benefits, he or she will be entitled to keep benefits accrued to date of leaving and under a defined benefit scheme they will be indexed. These are the "preservation rules".
- The tax rules allow a member to retire early if permanently incapacitated.
- A contracted-out defined benefit scheme must mirror a "model scheme". A minimum payment must be made to a contracted-out defined contribution scheme.
- Defined benefit schemes must provide limited inflation-proofing for pensions in payment and preserved pensions.

QUESTIONS AND ANSWERS

Q1 **To whom is the trustee's primary financial obligation?**

A The primary financial obligation of the trustees is to the members and their beneficiaries and the assets are held and managed by the trustees to give effect to the members'/beneficiaries' pension entitlements and rights.

Q2 **How is effect given to pension rights?**

A The cost of delivering those rights is met by investment and the management and the realisation of assets.

Q3 **Give four reasons why the cost of a DB scheme might increase.**

A 1. Poor investment returns.
2. Low interest rates/gilt yields.
3. Improved mortality.
4. Cost of regulation.

Q4 **What is meant by "balance of cost" in the context of a DB scheme?**

A The cost to the employer (after allowing for the member contribution) of ensuring 100% funding.

Q5 **What are the tax reliefs available to a registered scheme?**

A Within allowances:
- employer contributions are deductible
- employer contributions are not taxed on the member
- member contributions are relievable at marginal rates of income tax
- funds are free of UK tax on income and capital gains (although dividend credits cannot be reclaimed)
- generous tax-free lump sums are available on retirement and death.

Q6 **What is a pension credit member?**

A An individual who has been awarded a pension share on divorce.

Q7 **What are the statutory options open to a member who leaves after three months' service, but before two years?**

A The member may take a refund of personal contributions (less tax) or transfer benefits to another registered scheme.

Q8 **What is the lowest age at which a member can take benefits without them being treated as unauthorised payments?**

A 55 (lower if there is transitional protection or on grounds of ill-health).

Q9 **What is the condition for taking benefits early on grounds of ill-health?**

A The member must be unable to carry on his or her job because of ill-health or injury.

CHAPTER 2

Contributions

Sources

Contributions may be made to a pension scheme from a number of sources:
- the employer
- the member (employee or self-employed)
- an individual on behalf of the member
- HM Revenue & Customs (contracted-out personal pension schemes).

Furthermore, a personal contribution may be supplemented by tax relief.

There are essentially four areas of regulation.
1. Member protection: meeting the employer promise.
2. Stakeholder pensions and NEST.
3. Tax relief.
4. Contracting-out of the additional State pension.

Member Protection

Under a money purchase scheme, there is generally no obligation to pay a contribution or provide a predetermined level of retirement benefit (although the underlying investment may offer certain protections). The employer will pay a contribution, usually expressed as a percentage of pay which may supplement a member contribution. However, the employer can change the contribution from year to year subject to the impact on relations with employees. If a reduction or increase in contribution is substantial, the employer is expected to consult with employees (there is no formal definition of "consult").

It would be extremely unwise for employers to restrict themselves by promising a fixed contribution in the employment contract although the automatic enrolment rules to be introduced in October 2012 will require a minimum contribution.

There are provisions in the pension legislation, supervised by the Pensions Regulator, that require employer contributions to be paid when the employer has said that they will be paid. There are criminal sanctions (ultimately) on the employer that collects members' contributions from pay, but does not invest them in the member's pension.

The stakeholder pension rules required most employers of five or more employees to provide access to a designated stakeholder pension scheme or suitable alternative from October 2001, but no contribution was required unless the employer provides a group personal pension scheme in which case they are required to contribute at least 3% of pay. The automatic enrolment rules that are due to be implemented from 2012, will require employees to be enrolled automatically in the National Employment Savings Trust (NEST) or another qualifying workplace scheme (and the employee will have the chance to opt out).

When the automatic enrolment rules are implemented, the requirement to provide access to a stakeholder plan or suitable alternative will be withdrawn.

Contributions can only be paid to an occupational scheme if the scheme is established as a trust. The purpose is to ensure that when an employer, in particular, pays contributions to the scheme, that employer surrenders all control and any claims to ownership over the money. The trustees must operate a bank account to which the employer has no access.

If the scheme is a personal pension scheme, it may be established under trust or there may be a contractual relationship between the member and the scheme operator who owns the assets (typically a life assurance company) which again will deny access to an employer.

Defined benefit schemes are subject to the same restrictions as money purchase schemes, but there is an additional layer of rules under successive Pensions Acts to ensure that the employer makes a serious attempt to deliver the promise of a benefit calculated according to the scheme rules. Accordingly, the Pensions Regulator will wish to see that the scheme is funded adequately to meet its future liabilities (mainly benefits) and that where there is a shortfall, there is a "recovery plan".

Funding Requirements (Defined Benefit Schemes)

The funding requirements are necessarily complicated and are described here to give an idea of the strength of member protection.

The Maxwell scandal of the 1990s taught the legislators that regulation of long-term pension investment had to be pre-emptive.

Defined Benefit Schemes

The **Pensions Act 2004** introduced a *statutory funding objective* which was designed to address some of the shortcomings of the previous rules (minimum funding requirement or MFR).

The statutory funding objective is scheme specific and places an obligation on trustees to agree a strategy for meeting pension commitments with the sponsoring employer.

The objective is to ensure that there are sufficient and appropriate assets to cover technical provisions, reflecting the European Directive on the Activities and Supervision of Institutions for Occupational Retirement Provision (IORP). Technical provisions, in this context, means the amount necessary to cover liabilities, based on an actuarial calculation.

Although trustees or managers are to choose the method and assumptions appropriate for the calculation, they will have to abide by regulations and guidance produced by such bodies as the actuarial profession.

The trustees are required to prepare and maintain a statement of funding principles to ensure that the statutory funding objective is met. The written statement includes:

• funding objectives and the trustees' policy for ensuring that the objective is met
• arrangements for seeking the employer's agreement to funding
• implications of funding on scheme investment policy
• whether the Regulator has given directions on scheme funding
• methods and assumptions to be used in calculating technical provisions, and
• a period over which failure to meet the statutory funding objective will be rectified.

The statement must be reviewed at least every three years.

Trustees or managers must arrange for a written valuation of assets and technical provisions from the scheme actuary at least annually, although the valuations can be triennial if the trustees arrange for actuarial reports in the intervening years (or more frequently). The valuation must be made available to the employer within seven days of receipt. If the scheme had fewer than 100 members throughout a year, there is no need to issue a report or funding statement for that year.

In the case of multi-employer schemes where the scheme is segregated by employer and there is no cross-subsidy, each element is treated as a separate scheme for these purposes.

A summary funding statement must be issued to all scheme members within a reasonable time of the trustees receiving a valuation or actuarial report (three months). The statement should include an explanation for any change in the funding position and a number of other relevant matters.

The actuary's certificate must state whether the calculation of technical provisions: is in accordance with the prescribed principles; is consistent with prescribed guidance; and complies with any prescribed guidance. If the actuary cannot so certify, he or she must report to the Regulator within a reasonable period (10 days from the deadline).

A Code of Practice provides a list of matters relating to assumptions that should be covered by actuarial advice and discussed with the employer when assessing the technical provisions.

Codes of Practice are issued by the Pensions Regulator, which describes their function and status as follows.

The Pensions Regulator has a number of regulatory tools, including issuing Codes of Practice, to enable it to meet its statutory objectives. The Pensions Regulator will target its resources on those areas where members' benefits are at greatest risk.

Codes of Practice provide practical guidelines on the requirements of pensions legislation and set out the standards of conduct and practice expected of those who must meet these requirements. The intention is that the standards set out in the code are consistent with how a well-run pension scheme would choose to meet its legal requirements.

The Status of Codes of Practice

Codes of Practice are not statements of the law and there is no penalty for failing to comply with them. It is not necessary for all the provisions of a Code of Practice to be followed in every circumstance. Any alternative approach to that appearing in the Code of Practice will nevertheless need to meet the underlying legal requirements, and a penalty may be imposed if these requirements are not met. When determining whether the legal requirements have been met, a court or tribunal must take any relevant Codes of Practice into account.

The Code of Practice suggests an action plan and emphasises that trustees should monitor progress against it.

There is a requirement for the trustees or managers to prepare and maintain a schedule of contributions. The schedule must be agreed with the employer. The actuary must then certify the schedule. If the scheme is underfunded, the trustees and employer must agree on a recovery plan to bring the scheme to 100% funding.

If the valuation shows that the statutory funding objective is not met, the trustees or managers must put in place an appropriate (to the scheme) recovery plan which includes a timeframe. There are measures to review and revise a recovery plan. The plan must be sent to the Regulator within a reasonable period which the Code of Practice recommends is 10 days from certification by the actuary.

The schedule of contributions should also be sent to the Regulator within 10 days of certification.

The Code of Practice discusses the requirements of a recovery plan. It lists items which should accompany the plan when it is sent to the Regulator. It also includes suggestions of what may constitute contingent security: letter of credit, guarantee from another group company, securitised assets or an escrow account.

Trustees are expected to negotiate robustly with the employer, but to ensure that the employer is able to maintain the plan. The trustees are expected to make an assessment of the strength of the employer's covenant. A signed schedule of contributions (employer and member) must be agreed between trustees and employer which must list the rates and dates of those contributions. The schedule must be monitored by the trustees.

The scheme actuary should certify that the schedule of contributions is consistent with the statement of funding principles and that the objective is likely to be met. If the actuary cannot sign the certificate he must report that fact to the Regulator.

Where a contribution is not paid according to the schedule, the contribution becomes a debt on the employer. The non-payment should first be discussed with the employer. The trustees or managers, the actuary or the auditor will only be expected to report non-payment to the Regulator if they have reasonable cause to believe that failure is likely to be of material significance to the Regulator in the exercise of its functions.

The PA 2004 requires the trustees or managers to obtain the agreement of the employer: to any decisions about methods and assumptions to be used by the actuary in calculating technical provisions, to any matter to be included in the statement of funding principles and to any matter included in the schedule of contributions.

If no agreement is forthcoming, the trustees/managers may modify future accrual in order to secure the employer's agreement, such agreement to be recorded and members notified within one month. Failing agreement, the trustees/managers must notify the Regulator in writing and with further information listed in the Code of Practice within a reasonable time (10 days).

The trustees or managers will be obliged to seek actuarial advice when considering methods and assumptions to be used by the actuary in assessing technical provisions, preparing or revising the statement of funding principles, preparing a recovery plan or preparing or revising a schedule of contributions. The actuary will have to abide by prescribed requirements (such as guidance notes).

Where there has been failure to observe these requirements or agreement with the employer has not been forthcoming, the Regulator has a number of options:

- to modify future benefit accrual
- to give directions about how technical provisions should be calculated
- to give directions on how a failure to meet the statutory funding objective should be rectified
- to impose a schedule of contributions.

Note: If a UK scheme includes overseas members, the European Pensions Directive requires the scheme to be "fully funded" at all times. The regulations define this term as meaning that the scheme is required to have an annual valuation and any deficit is repaired within two years. The schedule of contributions must cover a two-year period. This is very onerous compared with the UK standard. If the technical provisions are not covered the trustees must send a valuation summary to the Regulator within a reasonable period (10 working days from the date the schedule of contributions is certified by the actuary.

The Regulator proposed triggers for filtering schemes before it would consider intervening:

- where the recovery period is longer than 10 years
- where the recovery period is less than 10 years, but the Regulator believes that the shortfall could be cleared more quickly given the funding target
- where the recovery plan is significantly "back-end loaded".

However, as a consequence of the consultation, the Regulator has said that the primary objective must be to get the "technical provisions right" on a prudent basis and this may mean a longer recovery period.

The Regulator will take into account the viability and credit rating of the employer. It will wish to know whether the trustees have investigated the financial strength of the employer and their independent advice.

Further guidance was published by the Regulator on 18 February 2009. In the context of a severe recession, the theme of the guidance was that "there is no reason why a pension scheme deficit should push an otherwise viable employer into insolvency". However, the main message was that employers will not be allowed to reduce contributions to underfunded defined benefit schemes in order to support dividends to shareholders.

The scheme funding provisions are central to the governance of defined benefit schemes. They are backed by the extensive powers of the Pensions Regulator to:

- investigate schemes
- require information to be disclosed
- freeze a scheme during an investigation
- ring-fence assets
- inspect premises
- require a skilled person's report
- recover unpaid contributions
- impose civil penalties
- issue orders, directions and notices
- appoint or disqualify a trustee
- modify future accruals
- direct how technical provisions could be calculated
- impose a schedule of contributions where the existing schedule is regarded as inadequate
- wind up a scheme
- act as an arbitrator between employer and trustees ("a referee not a player").

The **Pensions Act 2008** allows the Regulator to intervene if the technical provisions have been improperly assessed.

The period of a recovery plan will not usually exceed 10 years. Furthermore, as a consequence of each triennial valuation of scheme assets and liabilities, a contribution schedule will be drawn up and agreed between trustees and employer to which the employer must adhere. Each year, the scheme auditor must certify that contributions have been paid by the employer or give reasons why not.

When regulation of contributions was introduced in 1997, breaches of the regulations had to be reported to the regulator (the Occupational Pensions Regulatory Authority or OPRA, now superseded by The Pensions Regulator), but OPRA became so paralysed with trivial reports that contributions became subject to a Code of Practice after the 2004 Pensions Act. A Code of Practice is not law, but is very influential if a case comes to court.

There is a parallel set of rules for defined contribution schemes although they are less complicated.

Defined Contribution Schemes

The **Pensions Act 2004** (PA 2004) requires the trustees or managers of a defined payment scheme with more than one member to prepare and adhere to a payment schedule for each scheme year. The schedule must, as a minimum requirement, state what will be paid and when.

Within seven months of the scheme year end, the scheme auditor (who can be the company auditor) must provide a written statement to the effect that the contributions schedule has been adhered to, or if unable to do so, state why.

Contributions must be paid by the due date specified in the payment schedule. Member contributions must be paid within 19 days from the end of the calendar month when they were deducted from pay. AVCs are not required to be included in the schedule, but where they are, they are subject to the same reporting requirement.

The outstanding contribution becomes a debt on the employer 60 days after the due date. Section 269 PA 2004 provides that where there is a failure to pay a contribution in accordance with the payment schedule by the due date, and the trustees have reasonable cause to believe that the failure is likely to be of material significance to the Regulator in the exercise of its functions, then they must inform the Regulator within a reasonable period (defined in a Code of Practice) of the due date.

Examples of what is likely to be material are listed in the Code of Practice and include:

- where contributions are outstanding for 90 days from the due date unless delay is caused by an administrative error that is discovered after the 90 days and corrected immediately
- late payment due to dishonesty or misuse of assets

- where there is a failure to pay contributions which carries a criminal penalty such as fraudulent evasion of the obligation to pay member contributions
- where the trustees become aware that the employer does not have adequate procedures to ensure correct and timely payment
- where there is no early prospect of contributions being paid.

A delay beyond 90 days will not necessarily justify reporting. The Regulator will not expect a report in respect of a payment schedule affecting no more than four active members. Similarly, no report will be expected where there are short delays due to members joining or leaving for example, or where a claim has been made to the Redundancy Payments Service of the Department for Business, Innovation and Skills. It may be that trustees should report where there is a combination of otherwise non-reportable events.

According to the Code of Practice, the report should be made within 10 days of the trustees becoming aware of the material significance of the late payment. In exceptional cases, a report should be made earlier by telephone and then confirmed in writing.

If a report is made to the Regulator, then a report should also be made to members affected within a reasonable period. This is determined in the Code of Practice as within 30 days of the first report being made to the Regulator.

Trustees can be penalised by the Regulator for non-disclosure and employers for non-payment.

Main exemptions are one member schemes and insured earmarked schemes where all members are trustees and decisions are made by unanimous agreement.

An employer who deducts member's contributions from pay is required to pay that contribution to scheme trustees/managers within 19 days of the end of the month in which the deduction was made. Where there has been fraudulent evasion of the obligation this will be dealt with by the courts as a criminal matter.

The **Welfare Reform and Pensions Act 1999** introduced measures for personal pension (including stakeholder) contributions paid by an employer which reflect those relating to occupational schemes under the **Pensions Act 1995**. It states that the new rules will apply to any "direct payment" arrangements where contributions are paid on the employer's account or on behalf of an employee out of salary deductions.

Where an employee requests that contributions should be deducted from his or her pay and forwarded to a scheme by the employer, he or she must be provided with information about how the process will work, in writing and within two weeks of the request.

The information will cover:

- how does payroll deduction work
- how can he or she change a contribution
- how often will the employer change (the employer may refuse to change at intervals of less than six months under stakeholder rules).

Where an employer is asked to change a contribution within the rules, then it must do so no later than the next pay period.

The due date for employee contributions (ie the latest payment date) will be the 19th calendar day of the month following the month in which the salary deduction was made. The due date for employer contributions is the date agreed by the employer.

Note: A payment must be received by the due date.

The rate of contribution may be a cash amount or percentage of salary. It can be variable. Employer and employee rates must be shown separately.

Note: The record must be with the trustees or manager before the first due date.

It imposes an obligation on trustees/managers to monitor contributions under a direct payment arrangement. To this end the trustees/managers can request the employer to provide information on payments. The employer must comply within a reasonable time (the Code of Practice determines this as 30 days) after which the trustees/managers must inform the Regulator of non-compliance within a reasonable period (60 days of the formal request if the information is not due shortly).

If a contribution is not paid by a due date and the trustees/manager have reasonable cause to believe that failure is likely to be of material significance to the Regulator, they must report non-payment to the Regulator. A Code of Practice issued by the Regulator defines "material significance" and "reasonable period".

The trustee/manager must provide employees with information on the amount and dates of payments each year (possibly with the report of the trustees).

There are civil penalties for non-compliance reinforced by criminal sanctions if there is fraudulent evasion of a requirement to pay a contribution deducted from an employee's salary.

The Pensions Regulator has power to require documents, enter premises to inspect documents or question anyone in order to ensure compliance.

The requirements to notify the Regulator and members of late payment of contributions are the subject of a Code of Practice.

A delay beyond 90 days will not necessarily justify reporting. The Regulator will not expect a report in respect of a payment schedule affecting no more than four active members. Similarly no report will be expected where there are short delays due to members joining or leaving for example, or where a claim has been made to the Redundancy Payments Service of the Department for Business Innovation and Skills. It may be that trustees should report where there is a combination of otherwise non-reportable events.

According to the Code of Practice, the report should be made within 10 days of the trustees becoming aware of the material significance of the late payment. In exceptional cases, a report should be made earlier by telephone and then confirmed in writing.

New Schemes — NEST and Automatic Enrolment

Stakeholder Schemes and NEST

The stakeholder pension scheme was a new type of pension scheme, based heavily on rules that apply to Occupational Pension Schemes and Personal Pension Schemes. It was intended to offer wider choice and greater accessibility as the State pension and other social security benefits become increasingly targeted towards the "low paid" or those genuinely unable to earn. It also used the registration mechanism to introduce minimum standards, most noticeably in limiting the impact of charges.

There is no compulsion to contribute to a stakeholder pension scheme, but obligations are placed on an employer to provide access for employees.

Structurally there are two types of scheme: trust-based schemes whose regulation resembles that of occupational schemes, and those offered by a manager rather like a personal pension scheme. Stakeholder pension schemes rules are sponsored by the DWP (primarily concerned with member protection) and the Treasury (availability of tax relief and contracting-out). They are supervised by the Pensions Regulator and HM Revenue & Customs (HMRC) respectively.

The regulations require that no member should be required to make an investment choice. This means that while a choice may be offered, the scheme will have to offer a "default fund".

The stakeholder regulations require that where the member has made no choice as to how their fund is to be invested there must be a lifestyling option over the five years before retirement. The lifestyling option requires a phased movement of funds to less volatile investments.

A stakeholder pension scheme can refuse to accept payments of less than £20 (which is the "net" contribution if paid by a member). While these regulations allow broad access, it is worth mentioning that the general law prohibits discrimination on grounds of gender, race, age, disability or hours worked (ie part-timers).

The introducing legislation provided for charges to be limited on a stakeholder pension scheme. The mechanism used in the regulations is to prohibit any reductions in the value of members' funds other than where specifically allowed. The maximum charge was described as 1/365% of the fund value for each day that the investment is held by the scheme. From 6 April 2005, the daily charge cap increased to 3/730% for the first 10 years, reducing to 1/365 thereafter.

Auto-enrolment

At the heart of the **Pensions Act 2008** is the requirement for employers to provide automatic enrolment in a pension scheme to jobholders who are at least 22 years old but under state pension age, have earnings equal to or exceeding the income tax threshold, and are not already members of a qualifying scheme.

If an employee is below the age of 22 or has reached state pension age (but not 75) and wishes to join the scheme, the employer must contribute. If the employee is below the earnings threshold, the employer can choose whether to contribute.

The employer will usually have to enrol the employee within three months, during which time the employee will be given information about the scheme and the right to opt out. Auto-enrolment obligations on the employer will arise every three years (within three months before and three months after the anniversary), although the jobholder will have the option to leave the scheme.

Employees will have 30 days from the date they have become a member and received the information to opt out. They will then be entitled to a refund of contributions within 21 days or, if earlier, two pay days.

What makes the new model different from the stakeholder rules introduced from 2001 for employers is that employers will be required to pay a contribution or provide a benefit rather than simply offer the facility.

The contribution to a money purchase scheme must eventually be at least 8% of qualifying earnings made up of an employer contribution of 3%, a jobholder contribution of 4% and reinvested tax of 1% of qualifying earnings. Qualifying earnings are those falling between £5035 and £33,540 in 2006/07 terms, but these thresholds will be revalued with average earnings. The maximum contribution in a year is £3600 and this will increase with average earnings.

The minimum contribution requirements for defined contribution schemes will be phased over a period from October 2012 to February 2018. Employers will be assigned a date for starting automatic enrolment: larger employers will start before smaller employers and the smaller schemes will be staged according to PAYE reference. The "headline" contribution requirements are as follows.

	Employer contribution	Employee contribution (including tax relief)
October 2012	1%	1%
October 2017	2%	3%
October 2018	3%	5%

The employer has three options depending on the definition of earnings used. They are referred to as "tiers".

Tier 1 requires a contribution of at least 9% of the jobholder's pensionable pay. This includes an employer contribution of 4%.

Tier 2 requires a contribution of 8% of pensionable pay (this includes 3% from the employer) provided that the total pensionable earnings of all relevant employees to whom the tier relates adds up to 85% of their total remuneration.

Pensionable pay under Tiers 1 and 2 means basic pay or the employer's definition of pensionable pay if higher. Basic pay refers to non-variable remuneration. It need not include overtime, bonuses and commission, for example.

31

Tier 3 requires a contribution of at least 7% of the jobholder's total remuneration (3% employer contribution). So, all earnings must be pensionable.

The contribution will therefore be determined for a full year, rather than a pay period. What will matter is the value of the contribution being paid, not its method of calculation.

Defined benefit schemes will be required to pass a quality test that includes a member's pension of at least ¹⁄₁₂₀th of qualifying final pay (PA 2008 ss.20–28). This may be increased by the Secretary of State to ¹⁄₈₀th of qualifying pay.

Cash inducements to opt out

Late in the passage of the Bill through Parliament, the DWP added a clause that will prevent employers from offering inducements to employees to remain out of a qualifying workplace scheme (PA 2008 s.54). The DWP considered that inducements might include higher salaries and bonuses that may seem attractive in the short term, but less valuable over the longer term to retirement.

The ban will be supervised by the Pensions Regulator, who will have the power to enforce retrospective reinstatement in the scheme (with payment of arrears of contributions) and ultimately, financial penalties.

Operation of the National Employment Savings Trust (NEST)

The scheme created by the **Pensions Act 2008** is what is being referred to as NEST and this will operate under a trust. The trust will be run by the NEST Corporation (and member-nominated trustees), the members of which will, initially, be chosen by the Secretary of State.

The Personal Accounts Delivery Authority (PADA) was charged initially with overseeing the introduction of Personal Accounts. It was independent of the Government and, on 5 July 2010, its functions and assets transferred to the NEST Corporation and trustees of the new scheme. The objectives of PADA included:

• minimising the effect of the new rules on employer administration and existing schemes; and

• optimising participation by employees.

PADA published for consultation a number of proposals regarding payment of benefits. These now appear in the Scheme Rules and can be found on the DWP website.

1. The retirement income that will be available from between ages 55 and 75 may be provided by an annuity or income withdrawal

(described elsewhere, but essentially meaning that income is paid directly from the fund within certain limits). The open market option enabling the member to purchase the most suitable annuity available in the market will be available, but for those members who do not wish to access the open market, there will be a limited range of products on a focused choice panel of selected providers each of whom will have to meet the requirements of the scheme.

2. Members will be offered a range of funds. They may be specific funds chosen by the member, such as an ethical fund or the member may be invested in a "target date" fund. There are initially 45 target date funds, each designed to pay out a benefit in a different year. Each fund will therefore be structured according to its anticipated term (eg more cautious over the shorter terms).

3. The account will be able to provide 25% of accrued fund as a tax-free pension commencement lump sum and there will be trivial commutation options within current tax rules.

4. The rules will allow small pension funds to be combined by transfer at retirement.

5. Members will be offered an electronic self-service facility to make their retirement choices. Other media will also be available.

6. Information will be made available six months before age 65 (the nominal retirement age). More detailed information will be provided by the NEST Corporation between two and six weeks from retirement.

7. Members will be required to nominate those who should benefit on their death rather than express a wish. Beneficiaries are usually named in an expression of wish by the member and this avoids any exposure to inheritance tax. The trustees nominate the beneficiary after considering factors such as the member's wishes (that are very influential). This measure could therefore generate a liability to inheritance tax.

8. The member will be subject to the tax rules relating to registered pension schemes generally.

9. There will be two charges. There will be a daily charge on the fund that equates to one-third of one percent a year and a "one-off" charge of 1.8% on each contribution. The latter will be dropped when the scheme is more financially self-sufficient.

The 2010 Regulations ban transfers of cash equivalent lump sums into and out of NEST to ensure that the Scheme complements existing schemes. An exception is made for members who have reached normal minimum pension age (usually 55) or retire on grounds of ill health to enable funds to be combined. This restriction will be reviewed in 2017.

The requirement to provide a stakeholder facility (or suitable alternative) will be withdrawn.

Tax Relief on Contributions

An important feature of registered pension schemes is the tax relief available to contributions. The rules about tax relief are quite complicated although they are broadly the same for occupational and personal pension plans. The tax relief rules apply to employer and member contributions.

Employer contributions

Expenses that are wholly and necessarily incurred for the purposes of the trade may be deducted in calculating the amount of taxable profit that a business makes. There are similar rules for investment companies (expenses of management). Employer contributions to a pension scheme (not necessarily a registered scheme) will usually be treated as a necessary business expense in the same way as wages and salary.

In fact, when HMRC is assessing deductibility, it will consider the remuneration package as a whole and not necessarily the relationship between pay and pension contribution.

There is a great deal of law relating to what is and what is not deductible, but the general rule is that if HMRC considers that the remuneration is not incurred wholly and exclusively for the business, then part of it may be disallowed as a deduction. In particular, a deduction will not be allowed if HMRC considers that the main purpose of the contribution is to avoid tax.

If an individual controls a business, HMRC is unlikely to question what he or she is paid. However, if the individual employs a relative or close friend in the business, then HMRC will wish to ensure that the remuneration package is paid "at a reasonable rate" for the job rather than as a vehicle for transferring assets. HMRC may compare the job with that being undertaken by others in the same business and what they are paid.

In exceptional circumstances, the deduction may be "spread" over two or more years. This is when the employer contribution is unusually large in relation to its usual level.

As a general rule, the contribution will be spread to the extent that it exceeds 210% of the contribution paid in the previous chargeable period. There are exceptions, however. They are:

(a) where the amount of the excess relevant contribution(s) is less than £500,000

(b) where the contribution increase is intended to fund increases in line with the cost of living for pensions in payment

(c) where the contribution increase is intended to fund benefits for new employees.

The spreading rules are specific to a scheme, but relate to the employer's contribution as a whole. The figure is calculated by reference to aggregate contributions by the same employer in the chargeable period (usually accounting year). They ignore contributions paid by the member and are not calculated by reference to benefits provided for individual members. So, if a "special" contribution is paid to provide substantial past service benefits, it will make no difference to these rules if the benefits are being provided for one member or 10 members (for example).

Employer contributions are specifically not taxed on the member as a benefit if they are within the "annual allowance". If they exceed the annual allowance, they are taxed as a benefit at the member's marginal rate of income tax (after adding the excess to other income for these purposes) through the self-assessment process.

The Annual Allowance

The annual allowance is a personal allowance against which the aggregate of employer and member contributions for a tax year can be measured and assessed for tax. If contributions are within the allowance, they will not be taxed and will qualify for tax relief.

If the annual allowance is exceeded for a tax year, the excess will be taxed at marginal rates (even though it may have been allowed tax relief under a separate heading).

Example

Frances is a higher rate taxpayer who pays a personal contribution that enjoys full tax relief against her higher rate of income tax. She exceeds the annual allowance by £30,000. She will be assessed to tax at 40% of £30,000 = £12,000

> **Example**
> As above except that the contribution is paid by the employer. The employer is able to claim the contribution as a deduction for tax purposes, but the excess is assessed on Frances.

In respect of a money purchase scheme, the individual is able to choose "input periods" for the purposes of determining any allowance or liability. Second and subsequent input periods must end in the following tax year, but are not now limited to a 12 months maximum. Generally, no more than one input period may end in a tax year in respect of the same arrangement. For the purposes of applying the allowance, the member applies the relevant annual allowance to contributions paid in the input period ending in the tax year.

For a defined benefit scheme, the input period is determined by the scheme administrator.

> **Example**
> Bill has an input period that started on 1 August 2009 (the previous period ended the day before). The period could end no earlier than 6 April 2010 and no later than 5 April 2011. The annual allowance for any assessment period ending in the tax year 2010/11 was £255,000 and that was the aggregate input that could be made without liability to tax.

The input is more difficult to ascertain in respect of a defined benefit scheme because members do not have "earmarked pots and contributions". The legislation tells us to take the cash increase in pension over the year and multiply it by 16 (previously 10). So an increase of 1/60 of a salary of £60,000 would produce an input of £1000 × 16 = £16,000. Any lump sum not derived from commutation must be added at this stage. In doing this calculation, the increase in pension is derived from subtracting the pension and separate lump sum at the start of the year from the pension and separate lump sum at the end of the year. The figure at the start of the year may be increased with the CPI.

Obviously some items have to be ignored (pension credits on divorce, transfers to the scheme) and some items need to be added (pension debits, transfers from the scheme).

The annual allowance has fallen to £50,000 (in 2011/12) having started at £215,000 in 2006/07 and increased to £255,000 in 2010/11.

However, the member may carry forward unused allowance for any of the three immediately preceding tax years during which he or she was a member of a registered pension scheme (not necessarily an active member). Under this facility, unused allowance must be carried forward from the oldest year first. For these purposes, it is assumed that the annual allowance in 2008/09, 2009/10 and 2010/11 was £50,000. When relief is carried forward from 2011/12 or later, it must be used at the first opportunity.

Example			
Tax year	Annual allowance	Contribution paid	Unused allowance
2011/12	£50,000	£20,000	£30,000
2012/13	£50,000	£70,000	£10,000
2013/14	£50,000	£60,000	Nil

The scheme is required to pay tax an annual allowance charge over £2000 if the member requests it. The rules require the benefits under the scheme to be appropriately reduced. The scheme may offer the facility for tax charges up to £2000.

Eligibility for Tax Relief on Personal Contributions

Tax relief is available on personal contributions in the following circumstances:

- the individual is an active member of a registered pension scheme
- contributions are relievable pension contributions
- the individual is a relevant UK individual for the tax year.

The section defines the terms used.

Relievable pension contributions are contributions paid before a relevant UK individual is 75. For the purposes of this section, they include contributions paid by the individual and on behalf of the individual (including contributions paid to occupational schemes under the net pay arrangement), but excluding contributions paid by the employer and recovered from the employee's pay for the purposes of contracting-out (relievable under separate sections) and minimum contributions paid by HMRC in respect of contracting-out through a personal pension scheme.

The definition of a relevant UK individual for a tax year is:

- an individual with relevant UK earnings chargeable to income tax for that year
- an individual who is resident for tax purposes in the UK for part of the tax year

- an individual who has been UK resident for tax purposes at some time during the five tax years immediately before the contribution year and when the individual became a member of the scheme. This suggests that the member need not have joined the scheme within the previous five years
- an individual who has general earnings from overseas Crown employment subject to UK tax or the individual's spouse.

Earnings are not regarded as chargeable to income tax if they are not taxable in the UK by virtue of a double taxation agreement.

One of the biggest areas of simplification is the definition of relevant UK earnings which is made possible by introducing one tax regime for registered schemes. The definition includes:

- employment income. Earnings include basic pay, bonuses, overtime and commission from employment and chargeable
- chargeable income that derives from carrying on a trade, profession or vocation
- income which relates to patent rights in respect of inventions
- income from UK furnished holiday lettings
- general earnings from an overseas Crown employment subject to tax. If there are no such earnings the Crown employee may pay up to the basic amount (£3600 gross).

Redundancy payments are treated as employment income to the extent that they exceed the £30,000 tax-free amount.

The definition of relevant earnings specifically *excludes*:

- anything in respect of which tax was chargeable and which arose from the acquisition or disposal of shares or an interest in shares or from a right to acquire shares
- any payments on termination of employment in respect of which tax was chargeable (payments on termination of employment, etc)
- pensions in payment
- State benefits (including tax credits)
- earnings from international organisations such as the United Nations, which were exempt from UK tax.

Where the member is under the age of 18 (16 if in employment), the contract must be made by a parent or legal guardian. A contribution may be paid by a third party other than an employer, for convenience. There is no minimum age for membership of a registered pension scheme. If the member has no earnings, the maximum contribution will be £3600 (gross).

A number of parents, grandparents and husbands and wives of non-working spouses have made contributions for their children. There are allowances that can be used to prevent the contribution being a chargeable gift for inheritance tax purposes.

Annual Limit

The annual limit is the maximum aggregate personal contribution that can qualify for relief in the tax year. It is the greater of 100% of relevant earnings and £3600 (this latter limit previously known as the earnings threshold becomes the "basic amount"). The £3600 may be changed by Treasury Order (ie the Government). If the member has no relevant earnings the maximum is £3600 and eligibility would be based on tax residence. However, a contribution that exceeds 100% of earnings (up to £3600) is only allowable if the contribution can be collected by way of "relief at source".

The annual limit for relief is the greater of £3600 (before tax relief) and 100% of earnings.

Occupational Pension Schemes

For historical reasons, personal contributions to employer sponsored schemes are usually made on the net pay basis. Under this method the employer is responsible for paying the contribution and collecting it from the member's pay. The contribution is deducted from pay after National Insurance has been deducted, but before tax is applied. The consequence is that personal contributions are not relieved against National Insurance, but they are relievable against the highest marginal rate of income tax that would otherwise apply.

Since April 2006, the employer has been able to operate a net contribution basis as an alternative to the net pay basis.

Under the net contribution basis, the member pays the contribution net of basic rate tax (perhaps via the employer) and the scheme recovers the amount of the basic rate tax from HMRC. If the member is a higher rate taxpayer, the member's basic rate tax band is extended by the amount of the gross contribution. In so doing, the band of earnings subject to higher rate tax is reduced.

Employers may operate the net pay or net contribution basis, but must use the same basis for all members.

On rare occasions, the member may make a contribution without deducting relief at source (net contribution). The member then claims the relief from HMRC. This is known as relief on making a claim and might apply when the member pays an annual contribution at the end of a tax year that exceeds the remaining earnings from which it would otherwise be deducted.

Additional Voluntary Contributions, Additional Pension and Added Years

Occupational schemes usually offer the opportunity to top up benefits by way of a personal contribution (and until recently had to offer the facility). This is usually established as a money purchase option within the scheme and trust. The member is offered a choice of two or three investment media, but nearly always this is a link to an insurance company managed fund.

Public service schemes may offer the money purchase option, but may also offer the option to buy added years (now described as additional pension by some schemes). Under a scheme that offers a benefit calculated by reference to a rate of accrual multiplied by final pay and years of service, the added years facility invites the member to increase the number of years for a predetermined contribution that may be paid monthly or annually.

Added years are attractive and secure, but they are also quite expensive and offer reduced benefits if the member stops contributing before pension age for whatever reason. The new additional pension options express an amount of extra pension that can be purchased with the contribution. The problem with this option is that nobody knows what will be its purchasing power at retirement.

Salary Sacrifice

Personal contributions should not be confused with salary sacrifice. This is an agreement made with an employer and documented that requires the employer to pay a lower salary than the contractual amount and to redirect the saving to a pension scheme for the employee's benefit. The same principle can be applied to bonuses. The main requirement is that the sacrifice be agreed before the salary or bonus has actually been paid. A recent court case that applied VAT to some benefits derived from sacrificing remuneration has no application to pension contributions paid as a consequence of a sacrifice.

The reasons for sacrificing remuneration are:
- the member wishes to boost pension provision, and
- the sacrifice ensures that there will be no liability on the employee or employer for National Insurance contributions; personal contributions are paid after deduction of National Insurance (both options reduce the tax bill).

Remuneration sacrifice must be approached with caution:
- remuneration is reduced for all purposes, including the calculation of the State earnings-related pension
- it is also reduced for the purposes of underwriting financial products such as mortgages or permanent health insurance cover although some firms may be prepared to accept the figure before sacrifice.

Note: If an individual has income exceeding £100,000 the personal allowance is reduced by £1 for every £2 excess. There is a statutory basis of determining income for these purposes which allows the gross value of personal contributions to be deducted.

The impact of paying a personal contribution is therefore especially pronounced for an individual whose income is marginally more than £100,000.

Example

Nathan has income of £110,000. He decides to pay a personal contribution to a pension scheme of £10,000 (gross). He will actually pay £8000 and the balance of basic rate relief will be added by HMRC.

The £10,000 contribution can be deducted from income in determining whether the full personal allowance should apply. This reinstates £5000 or personal allowance which means that higher rate tax will be reduced by £2000.

Furthermore, total tax relief on the contribution will be 40% of £10,000 = £4000.

Total tax reduced is therefore £6000 or 60% of £10,000.

Key Facts

- As a general rule, there is no obligation on employers to contribute to a pension scheme. However, this will change with the introduction of automatic enrolment rules in 2012.
- Subject to the automatic enrolment rules, an employer can determine from year to year what to pay to a money purchase scheme.

- Under a defined benefit scheme, the employer is required to pay contributions adequate to meet the pension promise.
- The statutory funding objective is scheme specific and places an obligation on trustees to agree a strategy for meeting pension commitments with the sponsoring employer.
- The trustees are required to prepare and maintain a statement of funding principles to ensure that the statutory funding objective is met.
- The trustees or managers must obtain the agreement of the employer: to any decisions about methods and assumptions to be used by the actuary in calculating technical provisions, to any matter to be included in the statement of funding principles and to any matter included in the schedule of contributions.
- Trustees must prepare and maintain a contribution schedule which must also be agreed with the employer.
- If a regular valuation reveals a deficit, the trustees must also put in place a recovery plan to get the scheme to 100% funding.
- Automatic enrolment differs from stakeholder pension rules in requiring a contribution from employer and employee.
- Minimum contributions under the automatic enrolment rules will be phased from 2012.
- Employer contributions to registered pensions schemes are a deductible business expense if incurred wholly and exclusively for the purposes of the business.
- Deductibility for exceptionally large contributions may be spread for up to five years.
- The annual allowance is a personal allowance and is a measure in respect of total input from employer and employee.
- Relievable personal contributions may be made by a UK relevant individual who is not yet aged 75.
- The annual limit for relief is the greater of £3600 and 100% of earnings.
- Personal contributions to an occupational scheme are usually paid under the net contribution or net pay processes.
- Further information about implementing auto-enrolment schemes, and the relevant staging dates for different sizes of employer, is available at *www.thepensionsregulator.gov.uk/pensions-reform.aspx*.

QUESTIONS AND ANSWERS

Q1 Who can pay contributions to a registered pension scheme?

A
- Employer
- Member
- An individual on behalf of the member
- HMRC

Q2 What is the statutory funding objective?

A The statutory funding objective is scheme specific and requires trustees to agree a strategy for meeting pension commitments with the sponsoring employer. This means ensuring that the fund is adequate to meet its liabilities, most of which are benefits.

Q3 What is the statement of investment principles?

A The trustees are required to prepare and maintain a statement of funding principles to ensure that the statutory funding objective is met.

The written statement includes:
- funding objectives and the trustees' policy for ensuring that the objective is met
- arrangements for seeking the employer's agreement to funding
- implications of funding on scheme investment policy
- whether the Regulator has given directions on scheme funding
- methods and assumptions to be used in calculating technical provisions, and
- a period over which failure to meet the statutory funding objective will be rectified.

Q4 What is a recovery plan?

A If the valuation shows that the statutory funding objective is not met, the trustees or managers must put in place an appropriate (to the scheme) recovery plan which includes a time-frame (usually within 10 years). The objective is to ensure that the scheme is 100% funded against liabilities.

Q5 **What is the overall test of whether employer contributions are deductible?**

A The expense is necessary for the business (wholly and necessarily incurred).

Q6 **Describe the annual limit.**

A It is a limit on tax relief available to personal contributions.

Q7 **Describe the annual allowance.**

A It is a contribution allowance that applies to the aggregate of personal and employer contributions. Beyond the allowance the member pays tax on the excess (the annual allowance charge).

Q8 **How is higher rate relief given to contributions paid net of basic rate tax?**

A The basic rate tax band is increased by the amount of the gross contribution.

Q9 **Why should salary sacrifice be approached with caution?**

A It may reduce earnings for the purposes of calculating State pension and other State benefits.
It may reduce earnings for the purposes of mortgage applications and permanent health insurance.

CHAPTER 3

Personal Pension Schemes

Personal pension schemes are established and operated by a pension provider (also known as an operator or establisher). A pension provider is regulated by the Financial Services Authority. The key difference from occupational schemes is that they are not designed and established by an employer, although an employer may choose to contribute to a personal pension scheme as a means of providing a financial benefit for employees with the minimum administrative involvement.

The basic structure of a personal pension scheme is that an operator ("establisher") sets up a scheme and individuals are invited to join. Each individual ("member") is allocated an arrangement or group of arrangements that may be evidenced by a policy or plan. The operator will therefore rarely offer more than one or perhaps a handful of schemes, but each scheme may be subdivided into many arrangements.

If the scheme is offered by a life assurance company, the relationship between provider and members will usually be contractual (using a "deed poll" as a convenient legal tool for registering the member's interest). For some life assurance companies and other types of operator, the scheme will be established under one large trust (master trust): it will then resemble an occupational scheme albeit with slightly different personnel.

Personal pension schemes are always established on a money purchase basis and, until April 2012, will allow members to contract-out of the State earnings-related pension. Members of personal pension schemes are retail investors, even if contributions are paid by an employer, and protection is mainly provided by the Financial Services Authority and the Financial Services Compensation Scheme rather than the Pensions Regulator.

45

The tax rules for personal pension schemes are, with very few exceptions, mainly relating to investments and loans, the same as for occupational schemes. Like those schemes they must be registered to enjoy the full range of reliefs.

Personal pension schemes succeeded retirement annuity contracts. The latter were individual contracts between policyholders and life assurance companies (or friendly societies) that did not allow employer contributions or contracting-out. A key change brought about by personal pension schemes in the late 1980s was the facility to "unbundle" the services required by the scheme so the investment manager need not be the trustee, who need not be the operator, who need not be the administrator, for example.

Another big change implemented in 2006 was to establish one tax regime for all registered (tax privileged) schemes without distinguishing between personal and occupational schemes: the previous distinction allowed any significant funding of personal pension schemes while simultaneously accruing benefits under an occupational scheme, but this "barrier" has now been entirely removed.

Key Facts

- Personal pension schemes are established by operators and allow different services to be offered by different firms: they are unbundled.
- The tax rules for personal pension schemes are broadly the same as for occupational pension schemes since 2006.

CHAPTER 4

Contracting-out

The Basics

The basic premise of contracting-out is that the member (and his or her employer) pays a reduced rate of National Insurance, but surrenders entitlement to the additional State pension in order to provide a benefit through a private scheme. Legislation does not make this an easy option.

Defined Benefit Schemes

The decision to contract-out is made by the employer.

The employer and employee pay a reduced rate of National Insurance and the employer provides membership of an occupational scheme which meets the criteria of a "reference scheme". This is a theoretical defined benefit scheme. The employer will usually require an employee contribution as a condition of membership. The impact of the member's contribution is reduced by the National Insurance "rebate" (ie reduction) and the tax relief on the contribution.

Reference Scheme

The reference scheme is a model occupational scheme which provides benefits for members and surviving spouses.

Benefits for members are:
- a lifetime pension commencing at a normal pension age of 65, and
- an annual rate of pension of 1/80th of average qualifying earnings in the last three tax years preceding the end of service multiplied by years of service subject to a maximum of 40/80ths.

Benefits for surviving spouses are to be:
- a pension to commence on the day following death of the member whether or not this occurred before the age of 65
- where death occurs on or after normal pension age, a pension of 50% of the member's entitlement
- where death occurs before normal pension age 50% of the pension payable to a member had death occurred at normal pension age
- where the member died in deferment, the pension is to be revalued as though the member died after reaching normal pension age.

There is no requirement to provide a surviving spouse's benefit in the following circumstances:
- where the member marries after benefits have commenced, and
- where the surviving spouse remarries or where the surviving spouse cohabits at the time of death or subsequently.

Until 5 April 2009, "qualifying earnings" for the purposes of calculating these benefits were 90% of earnings falling between the lower earnings limit (the "qualifying earnings factor" or QEF) and the upper earnings limit, multiplied by 53. From 6 April 2009, qualifying earnings are limited by the upper accrual point in place of the upper earnings limit. "Normal pension age" is the earliest date from which a pension can be taken without actuarial reduction and as of right (ie without requiring permission from the trustees).

For benefit accrual before April 1997 and before the reference scheme test was introduced, the scheme was required to provide a pension that was at least equal to a guaranteed minimum pension (roughly a SERPS equivalent).

Money Purchase Schemes

The option to contract-out on a money purchase basis will be abolished on 6 April as will "protected rights".

Personal Pension Schemes

The option to contract-out via a Personal Pension Scheme was abolished on 6 April 2012.

Key Facts

- A defined benefit scheme may be contracted-out of the State second pension if it reflects a "reference scheme".
- DB schemes that were contracted-out before 1997 must provide a guaranteed minimum pension.
- Protected rights are abolished in 2012.

QUESTIONS AND ANSWERS

Q1   What is the basis of contracting-out?

A   The employer and member pay lower NIC. The member gives up entitlement to the additional State pension to benefit under a private scheme.

Q2   Who makes the decision to contract-out in a DB scheme?

A   The employer.

Q3   What is a GMP?

A   A guaranteed minimum pension is a minimum level of pension that must be provided in respect of pre-1997 contracted-out rights under a DB scheme.

Q4   Why does NIC not reduce for an individual who contracts-out under a personal pension scheme?

A   Employer and employee pay the full rate of NIC and HMRC redirects part of the contribution to the member's scheme.

CHAPTER 5

Authorised Payments

Condition of Tax Relief

Generous tax reliefs are allowed for registered pension schemes to encourage individuals and employers to put money aside for their retirement or for beneficiaries and dependants on the member's death. A condition of the tax relief is that no payments or implied payments are made from the scheme unless they are "authorised" by the tax legislation.

The legislation is specific about what payments are authorised and what are not. For example:

- there are specific rules about how and when retirement lump sum and income benefits may be taken
- there are specific rules about how death benefits may be paid and to whom
- there are rules about how small funds can be commuted and paid as a lump sum
- there are extensive rules about how the scheme can be invested (although the rules are not very restrictive and mainly aimed at preventing members enjoying a benefit that is inconsistent with the provision of retirement benefits)
- the rules allow loans to be made from the scheme within tight parameters subject to restrictions imposed by the member protection legislation
- the scheme is allowed to borrow within certain limits
- there are rules to prevent scheme assets being used to benefit the member or associates other than within the pension rules.

Authorised Lump Sums

Authorised lump sums (not necessarily tax-free) include:

- pension commencement lump sum
- serious ill-health lump sum: payable if a registered medical practitioner determines that the member's life expectancy is less than 12 months. The whole of the accrued benefit is payable as a tax-free lump sum if it is paid before age 75
- short service refund lump sum: payable if the scheme rules so allow when scheme service is less than two years when the member leaves. The refund is of personal contributions and is subject to income tax at a rate of 20% on the first £20,000 and 50% on the excess
- refund of excess contributions lump sum: if the annual limit in respect of personal contributions is exceeded, the member has the option of claiming a refund of the excess; no tax is payable
- trivial commutation lump sum: payable subject to very complicated rules; they require the payment not to exceed £18,000 from 2012/13; there are other clearly defined circumstances that allow small payments to be made (for example, payments made in error, "stranded pots" where a contribution is paid after a scheme crystallised)
- winding-up lump sum: payable on winding up when the value of rights does not exceed £18,000 from 2012/13
- lifetime allowance lump sum: payable when aggregate benefits exceed the lifetime allowance; the excess may be taxed at 55%, but can be paid as a lump sum.

There is a parallel list of authorised lump sums payable as death benefits.

These rules are complemented by rules in legislation sponsored by the Department for Work and Pensions (DWP) as part of the member protection framework. Occasionally, DWP rules impose further restrictions. So, for example, larger schemes are not allowed to make loans to the sponsoring employer. DWP contracting-out rules restrict the circumstances in which contracted-out rights can be paid as a lump sum.

There is nothing to prevent schemes transacting (renting, buying or selling) with members, but HMRC will wish to be sure that transactions take place on commercial terms and market values. For example, the scheme cannot pay an artificially inflated price for an asset as a means of encashing part of the fund without incurring a tax penalty. Similarly, a property held by the scheme cannot be let at less than a commercial rent if the tenant is, or is controlled by, a member.

There are particular restrictions on "investment-regulated" schemes investing in "taxable property". Investment regulated schemes are essentially schemes (personal or occupational) where one member and individuals connected with him or her is able to direct or influence how investments should be made.

Taxable property is "tangible moveable property" (ie property you can touch and move rather than, for example, financial instruments or buildings) or residential property (a definition of which would far exceed the space allocated here).

The taxable property rules were introduced quite late in the progress of the legislation in response to marketing initiatives that proposed putting holiday villas (residential property) in self-invested personal pension plans ("investment regulated schemes") for private use of the member (there were already rules to prevent personal use of assets, but they were ineffective and complicated). These initiatives were regarded by the legislators as being inconsistent with the primary objectives of a pension scheme Investment may be restricted whether it is direct or indirect (eg held by a company in which the scheme invests).

The taxable property rules can be quite restrictive for individuals who like to determine how their pension funds should be invested (self-invested personal pension plans or SIPP and small self-administered schemes or SSAS). They have no application to the larger schemes and funds where the investments are determined by professional and independent (of the member) fund managers.

Loans

Loans from pension schemes may be made under the tax rules without incurring unauthorised payment tax charges if they adhere to a narrow set of rules. HMRC and DWP rules are designed to balance investment freedom with protection of members and integrity of tax reliefs (to avoid abuse of reliefs).

Loans from a scheme to the sponsoring employer are generally not allowed under DWP member protection rules. Specifically exempted are loans where the scheme is restricted to directors.

Generally, employer-related investment should not exceed 5% of total scheme assets. Again there are exemptions for small schemes.

Small self-administered schemes are exempted from the restrictions on investment and loans subject to:
• all members being trustees; and

- where the rules of the scheme provide that before any investment of resources is made in an employer related investment, each member must agree in writing to the making of that investment.

A small self-administered scheme is defined in these circumstances as having less than 12 members.

An exception to the general restriction is also made for schemes that "earmark" directors' policies against which the loan can be secured.

Under the tax rules, loans may be made to any third party without the legislation imposing conditions if the borrower has no connection with the pension scheme. The connection in this context has a very wide meaning. It would be rare for an unconnected party to want to borrow from a scheme and similarly for the scheme trustees to wish to lend on appropriate terms.

If the loan is to an employer, then:

- the loan must not exceed 50% of the value of scheme assets
- the borrower must provide appropriate security for the loan
- the term of the loan must not exceed five years (although this may be extended in some cases where the loan cannot be repaid)
- the loan must be repaid in equal capital and interest instalments
- the interest rate charged must be based on an average of high street lending rates.

The employer loan rules were tightened in 2006 and are less attractive as a source of capital for the small or medium-sized business.

Borrowing

Small schemes may wish to borrow in order to purchase an asset or briefly to fund the purchase of a retirement vehicle. There are DWP restrictions and tax rules offer protection to the member and HMRC by requiring the borrowing to be on commercial terms.

The limit on borrowing is 50% of the net value (after other loans) of scheme assets. However, values will not be re-tested unless the loan is topped up.

Maximum "Top-up" Loan — Example

Value of plan (gross)   £200,000

Loan to scheme   £50,000

Maximum top up   50% of (£200,000 – £50,000) less outstanding loan = £75,000 – £50,000 = £25,000

If the maximum is exceeded, there will be a liability to a scheme sanction charge on the excess.

Unauthorised Payments and Tax

There is a range of tax charges on unauthorised payments and even on the income that may derive from unauthorised investments. Just as important as the amount of the charge is where it falls.

Unauthorised payment charge

This is a tax on the member at a rate of 40% of the value of the payment.

Unauthorised payment surcharge

If the payment represents at least 25% of the value of the fund (attributable to the member), there will be an additional 15% charge on the member (ie total charge of 55% on the member).

Scheme sanction charge

This is a charge on the administrator of the scheme and this means that it will be taken from the member's fund. It will be at a rate of 15% if the unauthorised payments charge has been paid and is payable in addition to the charges above. There are a few instances where there is a chargeable payment even though there are no unauthorised payment charges. An example is where rent and capital gains are derived from an unauthorised investment in taxable property. The rent does not diminish the value of benefits (quite the contrary), but to discourage the transaction, tax is charged on rent or deemed rent, similarly on capital gains on selling the asset. In these circumstances, the scheme sanction charge is 40%.

Deregistration charge

There may be instances where more than 25% of the value of scheme assets represents an unauthorised payment or there has been a breach of the HMRC disclosure rules and HMRC exercises its power to deregister the scheme. In addition to the above charges, there will be a deregistration charge of 40% of the value of scheme assets immediately before deregistration.

Key Facts

- Payments from a registered scheme must be authorised.
- Not all authorised lump sums are tax-free.
- There are restrictions on investment regulated schemes investing in taxable property.
- Registered pension schemes may make loans although loans to the sponsoring employer are more heavily regulated.
- A registered pension scheme may borrow up to 50% of the net value of assets.
- The tax incurred by a scheme making an unauthorised payment may fall on the administrator and the member.

QUESTIONS AND ANSWERS

Q1   **What is the fundamental requirement for a member to sell assets to his or her pension scheme?**

A   The transaction must take place on commercial terms.

Q2   **What is an investment regulated scheme?**

A   A scheme where a member or individuals connected with the member are able to influence how funds are invested (ie the assets).

Q3   **What is taxable property?**

A   Residential or tangible moveable property.

Q4   **What is the general rule regarding schemes lending to employers?**

A   It is not allowed (an exception is made for small occupational schemes).

Q5   **What is the maximum that a scheme can borrow?**

A   50% of the net value of scheme assets.

CHAPTER 6

Retirement Benefits

Authorised Payments

The primary objective of a pension arrangement is to provide an income for life from a pension age. The legislation used to refer to providing an income in old age, but the expression has been overtaken by improved mortality and changing attitudes.

The member may choose at what age to take the pension, but any payment made outside the parameters set by the tax legislation (when, how much and to whom) for registered pension schemes will be taxed heavily as an unauthorised payment.

The tax legislation specifies that benefits may usually be taken from a normal minimum pension age of 55. There are some variations on these parameters:

- where occupational scheme arrangements were established prior to 12 December 2003, they may retain a normal minimum pension age of 50 for individuals who were members at 5 April 2006, and
- where the member was a member of a special occupation before 6 April 2006 that allowed an early pension age (such as certain sportsman and musicians), the member may retain that early pension age. Some occupations were permitted an age as low as 35
- should the member become permanently incapable of continuing his or her normal occupation because of illness or accident, he or she may take the pension at any age
- should the member's life expectancy be restricted by injury or illness to no more than 12 months, he or she may take the value of the pension as a tax-free capital sum whatever the age.

The process of becoming entitled to benefits (and some other transactions) is known as "crystallisation".

However, if a member reaches the age of 75 without having crystallised benefits, the uncrystallised funds are subject to a Benefit Crystallisation Event although benefits may not actually be taken at that time.

Benefit Crystallisation Events (BCE)

The pension tax legislation is built on a framework of allowances. There are few prohibitions. If the allowances are exceeded, legislation imposes additional tax charges. We have seen that if the input (contribution) allowances are exceeded, there will be a tax charge.

There is also a control, the lifetime allowance, over output. If the lifetime allowance is exceeded, the member is subject to a lifetime allowance charge. This is not an unauthorised payment charge.

Pension arrangements are measured against the lifetime allowance whenever there is a Benefit Crystallisation Event (BCE). This would typically be when retirement or lump sum death benefits are taken, but could be on other events such as when funds are moved outside the UK regime and transferred to a Qualifying Recognised Overseas Pension Scheme (QROPS).

The full list of BCEs is:

Benefit Crystallisation Event	Description
1. Designation of money purchase arrangements as available for the payment of drawdown pension.	Drawdown refers to taking a variable income directly from the accumulated fund. It may be capped or flexible drawdown.
2. The individual becoming entitled to a scheme pension.	Scheme pension is described elsewhere, but again is an income payable directly from the fund. It is the only pension available from a defined benefit scheme. The pension is determined by the trustees who are responsible for meeting the obligation.

58

3. A scheme pension in payment increases by more than a threshold rate and permitted margin.	Increases are allowed within tight parameters to protect real values against inflation.
4. The individual becoming entitled to a lifetime annuity purchased by the fund.	An annuity is an agreement by a life assurance company to pay an income for life and payable yearly or more frequently. The annuity will usually be guaranteed (and may include options such as death benefits and inflation protection), but may be linked to an investment fund or index.
5. The individual becoming entitled to a pension or lump sum from a defined benefit scheme for the first time on reaching age 75.	
5a. The individual reaching the age of 75 having designated sums or assets held for the purposes of a money purchase arrangement under any of the relevant pension schemes as available for the payment of drawdown pension to the individual.	
5b. The individual reaching the age of 75 having sums of assets held for the purposes of a money purchase arrangement under any of the relevant pension schemes".	
6. The individual becoming entitled to a lump sum.	To the extent of the lump sum.

7. An individual becoming entitled to a lump sum death benefit.	To the extent of the lump sum. Taking an income death benefit is not a BCE and the benefit is not measured against the lifetime allowance.
8. Transfer of rights to a qualifying recognised overseas pension scheme (QROPS).	A transfer to a scheme that is not a UK registered scheme or a QROPS is an unauthorised payment and taxed very heavily.
9. Other events prescribed in regulations.	

At each BCE, the cumulative value of benefits crystallised is measured against the lifetime allowance. Any excess is subject to the lifetime allowance charge at a rate of 55% (lump sums) or 25% not paid to the member or beneficiary as a lump sum. Income may be subject to further tax charges such as the normal rates of income tax applicable to pensions in payment.

Example

The lifetime allowance was £1.5 million in 2006/07.

The lifetime allowance was £1.8 million in 2010/11.

Jill crystallises benefits on 1 September 2006. The value of those benefits is £750,000 and this is 50% of the lifetime allowance in 2006/07.

In 2010/11 she considered crystallising more benefits and wondered how much was available before breaching the lifetime allowance.

In 2010/11, 50% of the lifetime allowance remained. In 2010/11 this equated to benefits to the value of 0.5 x £1.8 million = £900,000.

If the benefits were taken in 2010/11 as pension and lump sum, the lump sum would have been tax-free and the pension would have been taxed as non-savings income if they did not exceed £900,000 in total.

In calculating the value of benefits being crystallised, the value of the fund is usually used under a money purchase scheme. Under a defined benefit scheme the pension is converted to a lump sum for these purposes by application of a factor of (usually) 20: a pension of £10,000 converts to a value of £200,000 for these purposes. In a very few cases agreed with HMRC and where the rate of pension indexation is unusually generous, the factor may exceed 20.

If some benefits were taken before 6 April 2006, they must be taken into account at the first BCE after that date. The value of pre-2006 benefits is derived by multiplying the pension by 25 and ignoring any lump sum previously taken.

The standard lifetime allowance was set at £1.5 million in 2006/07 and was indexed until 2010/11 from when it was frozen at £1.8 million. Where substantial benefits had accrued prior to 6 April 2006, they may be subject to transitional protection (primary or enhanced protection) which allows the lifetime allowance to be modified and based on values at that date.

From 6 April 2012, the standard lifetime allowance will reduce to £1.5 million. However, individuals who run the risk of exceeding this allowance because they were targeting benefits within the £1.8 million allowance may give notice to HMRC (by 5 April 2012) that an "underpinned" lifetime allowance of £1.8 million should be used for these purposes if it is higher than the standard lifetime allowance. This is known as "fixed protection" and should be claimed on an HMRC form (APSS 227). They will then be subject to restrictions that:

- require there to be no further benefit accrual (and no further contributions to a money purchase scheme) or
- require no new arrangements to be opened except for the purpose of accepting transfer values and/or
- limit the types of transfer that can be made from the arrangement.

Taking the Pension Commencement Lump Sum

The tax legislation also allows the member to convert some of the pension to a tax-free pension commencement lump sum (tax-free lump sum). Broadly speaking, this must represent no more than 25% of total benefits being crystallised (entitlement must arise at the same time as the pension is taken and the payment must be made in the period starting six months before the pension is paid and 12 months after) although measuring the limit under a defined benefit scheme can be problematic.

The Government has suggested that it may allow the lump sum to be taken at any time, but there is no immediate prospect of this progressing beyond discussion and consultation.

The proportion may be larger in respect of benefits that accrued under an occupational scheme before 6 April 2006.

Lump Sums Under Defined Benefit Schemes

The pension rules generally restrict the pension commencement lump sum to 25% of the value of benefits. Under a money purchase scheme where the member accumulates a fund that is then converted to benefits, for example, by purchase of an annuity, the calculation is straightforward: it is 25% of the accumulated fund.

However, under a defined benefit scheme, the benefit is expressed as a pension, not a fund. The value of benefits is calculated as 20 times the pension for tax purposes. However, in deriving the lump sum, account also has to be taken of the rate at which the scheme converts pension to lump sum (commutation rate). This will vary with interest rates and is determined by the trustees on the advice of the scheme actuary.

The formula used by HMRC for determining the lump sum is:

$$\frac{P \times CF}{1 + (0.15 \times CF)}$$

Where P is the annual pension and CF is the commutation factor.

If the commutation factor is 12 and the pension before commutation is £100,000, the maximum lump sum under HMRC rules (without incurring unauthorised payment charges) is:

$$\frac{£100,000 \times 12}{1 + (0.5 \times 12)} = \frac{£1,200,000}{2.8} = £428,571$$

It is unusual for a member not to take the lump sum even if the primary requirement is for income. The lump sum can be invested for income. The reasons are:

- the whole entitlement is paid "up front" unlike the accompanying pension (so it is not dependent on survival)
- the whole of the lump sum is tax-free and if used to purchase a purchase life annuity, most of the annuity instalment will be tax-free (unlike a pension annuity).

The **Finance Act 2011** requires that under a money purchase scheme, uncrystallised benefits should be measured against the lifetime allowance at age 75, but that benefits need not be taken until nominated by the member or on death. The pension commencement lump sum must still be taken within 6/12 months of the entitlement to the related pension arising. The age of 75 becomes less significant although as a threshold it will determine what tax will apply on death and serious ill-health. Lump sum death benefits payable after age 74 will be subject to tax at 55%.

The pension is taxed as "non-savings" income. It is therefore subject to income tax which is deducted before payment by the scheme administrator. The whole of each instalment is subject to tax. Although pension income is treated in a similar way to earned income, it is not subject to National Insurance and neither will it support further contributions to a pension scheme.

The pension deriving from a money purchase scheme is often provided by a pension annuity. The annuity is purchased with the member's accumulated fund and is usually selected by the member under the "open market option". Pension annuities are also known as compulsory purchase annuities because at one time, the annuity was the only way in which the benefit could be provided.

Purchase life annuities are not pension annuities. They allow any individual to purchase an income which is not subject to the same restrictions as a pension annuity. Furthermore, purchase life annuities are taxed differently:

- part of each instalment (capital content) is treated as a return of the purchase price and is not taxed — this part increases with age at date of purchase
- the balance of the instalment (interest element) is taxed as investment income.

There are certain restrictions and conditions on pensions in payment:

- they must be payable for life
- they must be payable in at least annual instalments
- they must be non-assignable although they may provide a pension for a dependant on the death of the member and may also be paid for a "term certain" (a guaranteed minimum period)
- scheme pensions may not reduce except in certain defined circumstances such as when a member reaches State pension age under a bridging pension or when a member is able to stop an ill-health pension
- scheme pensions may only increase within certain tightly defined parameters.

What is an Annuity?

An annuity is a contractual obligation to pay an income for a specific term (that may be a lifetime or joint-lifetime). The annuitant pays a lump sum to a life assurance company and the life assurance company pays the income. The income may be guaranteed or it may be variable and linked to the performance of an investment fund.

The rate of income is determined by:

- the term of the annuity and for how long instalments will be paid
- the yield on underlying investments. Guaranteed annuity payments will be secured primarily by investment in fixed interest assets such as gilts
- prevailing interest rates that will help to determine the gilt yield
- the mortality risk of the annuitant, itself based on age, health and lifestyle
- the costs of administering the annuity.

The annuity rate is primarily derived from dividing the purchase price plus net investment returns by the term over which it is to be paid. However, by "pooling" investments it is possible to enhance the rate by means of a mortality gain.

The mortality gain is an enhancement to the fund after allowing for some annuitants dying before they were expected to. So, to use an extreme example, if an individual purchased an annuity (without any death benefit) for £100,000, but died the next day and before entitlement to any instalment, the £100,000 will accrue to the fund for the benefit of other annuitants. Mortality gain increases with age so is an important feature of pension annuities.

The annuity may include a number of different options:

- increasing: it may increase at a fixed rate or in line with an index such as an inflation index
- variable: the annuity fund is linked to a fund or investment index which may go up or down in value with a consequent impact on the income payable
- guarantee: this does not refer to the level of payment so much as a minimum payment term (sometimes called a "term certain"): the annuity will pay for the term even if the annuitant dies within that term. The maximum guarantee allowed on a pension annuity is 10 years
- joint-life: the term is the lives of the pensioner and his or her spouse or civil partner. The annuity stops on the second life to die

- annuity protection: in the event of death, the annuitant's estate receives a lump sum representing the purchase price of the annuity less instalments paid.

Each of the options comes at a price and the annuity rate will reduce accordingly. Some providers will increase the rate for individuals whose life expectancy is impaired by ill-health or lifestyle (such as smoking).

A recent addition to the market is the "short term annuity". This is available to drawdown pension arrangements and allows the arrangement, on the advice of the member, to purchase an annuity for up to a five-year term in order to provide withdrawals. The annuity must not exceed the drawdown limits. The purpose of the short-term annuity is to provide a secure income during a short investment period when investment values are likely to be volatile.

What is a Scheme Pension?

We have already seen that under a money purchase scheme, the member accumulates an identifiable fund which may be used to purchase an annuity at pension age. The amount of pension will be determined by the size of the fund and the rate of conversion to income. It may also be applied to providing an unsecured pension.

The annuity will usually provide a guaranteed income for the life of the member or for the joint lifetimes of the member and a spouse or registered civil partner. It is chosen by the member who, in effect, instructs the trustees or scheme manager to purchase an annuity in his or her name (a lifetime annuity) from a life assurance company. The life assurance company becomes responsible to the member for meeting the contractual payments.

Under a scheme pension, the benefit is expressed as an income and it is for the trustees or manager to meet the obligation to provide the income using whatever scheme resources are necessary. The amount of the pension is determined in accordance with the scheme rules which, in the case of a defined benefit scheme, will provide a formula for the calculation such as $\frac{1}{60}$th of final salary for each year of service.

Example

Harry is a member of a defined benefit scheme that provides a pension of ¹⁄₆₀th of final pensionable salary for each year of service. He retires in January 2011 having completed 30 years as an active member of the scheme. His final salary is calculated according to the scheme rules as £90,000.

He will retire on a pension of $30 \times 1/60\text{th} \times £90,000 = £45,000$

Note: For the purposes of measuring the capital value of the pension against the lifetime allowance, the pension is multiplied by 20 (see above) ie $20 \times £45,000 = £900,000$ (50% of the lifetime allowance of £1.8 million in January 2011).

The trustees may decide to provide the pension directly from scheme assets or they may simply purchase an annuity from a life assurance company to provide the income. Where the annuity is purchased, it remains an asset of the scheme and the trustees remain responsible albeit indirectly for the income payments.

All defined benefit pensions are scheme pensions and some money purchase pensions. Money purchase schemes usually offer the open market annuity option which is mutually exclusive of scheme pensions. Under a money purchase scheme, the amount of pension is not usually determined until benefits are actually taken.

Drawdown Pensions

Various names have been given to drawdown pensions including pension fund withdrawal and income drawdown. It refers to an option that allows the member to take varying withdrawals directly from the fund from year to year, but subject to a maximum. The maximum withdrawal is reset at least every three years (five years if the "reference period" started before 6 April 2011). The fund may purchase a short-term annuity in the name of the member to provide a "stable income" for up to five years.

The attraction of the drawdown option, which is only available to money purchase schemes, is that it offers flexibility and a lump sum death benefit.

However, there are drawbacks and qualifications. For example:

- the expense loading will usually be higher than for an annuity (the main competition)

- the fund may only provide limited certainty about future investment returns
- the fund is not pooled, unlike an annuity fund so there is no mortality gain in anticipation of some members dying prematurely. This means that the fund must "work harder" to match an annuity (to follow the logic through, that suggests a higher risk investment which itself implies that in making a comparison, the drawdown pension should carry a risk premium).

Nevertheless, the drawdown fund may purchase an annuity or convert to a scheme pension. Drawdown pensions are payable to any age, but from age 75:

- the maximum withdrawal must be reviewed every year
- there is a test against the lifetime allowance at age 75 (a BCE), but no further tests beyond that.

From 6 April 2011, there are two types of drawdown available. Capped drawdown resembles the facility available before that date, but flexible drawdown places no restriction on the maximum withdrawal that may be taken in a year.

Flexible drawdown requires the member to declare that they can meet a "Minimum Income Requirement" (MIR) when they choose the option. The requirement is £20,000 and only the following types of income may be counted towards it:

- a state pension
- a scheme pension paid as an annuity
- a scheme pension that is not paid as an annuity from a scheme that has at least 20 pensioner members
- a lifetime annuity or dependant's annuity under a registered pension scheme that will remain level or can increase in payment
- a variable lifetime or dependant's annuity where the income only follows the RPI or if it does not, the minimum income payable
- an overseas pension that would fall under the above headings if from a registered pension scheme. Overseas pensions have a specific meaning
- benefit payments from the Pension Protection Fund
- other state or overseas state pensions (such as war pensions)
- pensions payable from, or in anticipation of, payments from the Financial Assistance Scheme.

As well as the member having to declare that he or she meets the MIR, they must also make a declaration that no contributions have been made earlier in the tax year. If contributions are made after flexible drawdown comes into operation, they will be treated as exceeding the annual allowance.

Recycling the Tax-free Lump Sum

Within generous allowances, the pension commencement lump sum is tax-free. As the rules were originally implemented if it were to be reinvested as a personal contribution, it would be supplemented by basic rate tax under the relief at source regulations (that would add another 25% to the investment). Furthermore, the high income investor could have claimed higher rate relief against the grossed up contribution.

The option is not as attractive as it may seem for most individuals because for every £1 of lump sum taken from a scheme, a further £3 must be converted to pension and taxed. For some arrangements that were established before 2006, the available lump sum may be more than 25% of the total value.

Nevertheless, legislation now restricts how much lump sum may be reinvested without incurring unauthorised payment charges (particularly severe given that the lump sum would otherwise have been tax-free). HMRC is given wide powers to link a contribution to a lump sum that has been paid or will be paid in the future.

The recycled lump sum will be an unauthorised payment if:

- the member receives a pension commencement lump sum
- the level of contribution to a registered pension scheme is therefore significantly increased (usually by 30%)
- the additional contributions are paid by the member or somebody else such as the employer
- the recycling was pre-planned at a "relevant time". Pre-planning may occur when the lump sum is paid (the relevant time) or when the increased contribution is paid in anticipation of receiving the lump sum (also the relevant time)
- the amount of aggregate pension commencement lump sums over a 12-month period exceeds 1% of the lifetime allowance
- the cumulative amount of additional contributions exceeds 30% of the pension commencement lump sum. In determining what is cumulative, the rule requires each contribution above the "base amount" to be aggregated.

The recycling rule will not apply if the increased contribution is attributable to remuneration sacrifice, redundancy, sale of investments or use of savings.

If the recycling rule applies, the amount of the lump sum (excluding any amount subject to the lifetime allowance charge) is deemed to be an unauthorised payment. This means that it would be subject to the unauthorised payment charge at 40%. In theory, there may also be an unauthorised payments surcharge of a further 15%. There would ordinarily be a scheme sanction charge on the administrator.

An unauthorised payment charge will usually attract a scheme sanction charge on the administrator, but this may be avoided if the administrator is able to demonstrate reasonable grounds. This might include the administrator having asked the member if the lump sum was to be part of a recycling exercise.

Key Facts

- The main control over output is the lifetime allowance.
- Arrangements are measures against the lifetime allowance whenever there is a Benefit Crystallisation Event.
- At each BCE, the cumulative value of benefits crystallised is measured against the lifetime allowance. Any excess is subject to the lifetime allowance charge at a rate of 55% or 25%.
- The pension is taxed as "non-savings" income.
- Annuities must be payable for life in at least annual instalments.
- A scheme pension is determined by the trustees in accordance with the scheme rules rather than by a life assurance company as is the case with an annuity.
- Drawdown pension offers a variable income drawn directly from the fund
- There is no mortality gain with a drawdown pension so the fund has to "work harder" to match an annuity.
- If a significant pension commencement lump sum is reinvested in a registered pension scheme, the lump sum will be taxed as an unauthorised payment under the recycling rule.

QUESTIONS AND ANSWERS

Q1   What is the significance of a benefit crystallisation event?

A   It triggers a valuation of aggregate benefits against the lifetime allowance.

Q2 **Why might an individual be persuaded to take the pension commencement lump sum even though it will reduce the available pension?**

A The whole entitlement is paid "up front" unlike the accompanying pension (so it is not dependent on survival); the whole of the lump sum is tax-free and, if used to purchase a purchase life annuity, most of the annuity instalment will be tax-free (unlike a pension annuity).

Q3 **How are purchase life annuities taxed?**

A Part of each instalment (capital content) is treated as a return of the purchase price and is not taxed. This part increases with age. The balance of the instalment (interest element) is taxed as investment income.

Q4 **Under the drawdown option how frequently must the maximum withdrawal be reviewed?**

A The maximum withdrawal is reset at least every three years (five years if the last review was before 6 April 2011).

Q5 **What percentage of the lifetime allowance must aggregate lump sums exceed if they are to be subject to the recycling rule?**

A The recycling rule may apply if the amount of aggregate pension commencement lump sums over a 12-month period exceeds 1% of the lifetime allowance.

Q6 **What are the "penalties" if the recycling rule applies?**

A If the recycling rule applies, the amount of the lump sum (excluding any amount subject to the lifetime allowance charge) is deemed to be an unauthorised payment. This means that it would be subject to the unauthorised payment charge at 40%. In theory, there may also be an unauthorised payments surcharge of a further 15%. There would ordinarily be a scheme sanction charge on the administrator (15%).

CHAPTER 7

How Safe is My Pension?

Background

Membership of a defined benefit occupational pension scheme used to require a "leap of faith" on the part of its members. They were invited to join and contribute to a scheme that promised a benefit possibly 20 or 30 years hence. Yet even with the best intentions, many events could conspire to thwart the delivery of the promise: the value of assets could fall, the cost of providing benefits could increase, the sponsor could fail, to name but three.

High profile schemes and employer failures in the 1990s persuaded the legislators that what law there was had become unfit for purpose. Much of the legislation represented little more than platitudes with very little sanction or enforceability.

Radical change was introduced by the **Pensions Act 1995** and this was itself streamlined and reinforced by the **Pensions Act 2004**. In parallel, the **Financial Services and Markets Act 2000** introduced powerful regulation of packaged investments and the investment markets.

Occupational pension schemes are now subject to the following.

- Trust law: any scheme must be written under trust if it is to accept funding payments. Trustees are required to be accountable and act solely in the financial interests of the beneficiaries (in this case, members and their dependants). Broadly speaking they may not benefit from the trust unless specifically allowed to do so, for instance because they qualify as a member.
- Pensions Acts and supporting regulations provide a framework of scheme governance and member protection.

- The **Financial Services and Markets Act 2000** (FSMA 2000) regulates investments, investment markets and the administration of personal pensions.
- HM Revenue & Customs supervises the tax and tax reliefs applicable to pensions.
- The Department for Work and Pensions that supervises contracting-out and sponsors member protection legislation.

The main regulatory bodies, apart from the courts are:

- the Pensions Regulator; the Regulator is much more proactive and has much wider powers than its predecessor until 2005, the Occupational Pensions Regulatory Authority (itself only established in 1997)
- the Financial Services Authority established under the FSMA 2000.

In the event that the employer becomes insolvent the member is further protected by:

- winding-up rules explaining how assets must be applied to the provision of benefits
- the Pension Protection Fund that offers support for benefits if the scheme is unable to meet its financial obligations; for corporate insolvencies from 1997–2005, the scheme may be supported by the Financial Assistance Scheme.

The Trust

The main structural protection for members is the requirement for all funded occupational schemes to be written subject to a trust. Trusts are a peculiarly British legal concept that separates the legal ownership of property from the right to enjoy the use of that property or the income from it. Trusts offer security and qualify the scheme for tax relief.

In the context of pension schemes, the trustees are required to:

- collect and invest contributions and other input
- manage the investments by balancing the twin objectives of maximising the return and protecting the capital
- pay the right benefit (in accordance with the scheme trust deed and rules) to the right members or beneficiaries at the right time.

They also have a number of statutory duties including accounting for tax.

The primary duty of the trustee is the one of carrying out the function entrusted to the person whether as an individual trustee, a member of a committee of management or a director of a trustee company, with the utmost good faith. The trustee must:

- at all times be impartial and bear in mind that the duty is solely to the beneficiaries of the scheme
- remember that he or she is not a representative of anybody and his or her personal opinions are of no consequence in determining the appropriate actions that he or she is required to perform for the beneficiaries
- perform his or her duties diligently and act as a prudent "man" of business using common sense and relying upon expert, professional advice as and when necessary in order to assist him or her in reaching a proper conclusion.

If he or she is proved not to have acted in good faith, he or she may be liable personally for any loss to the beneficiaries.

In discharging these duties, the trustees must observe specific requirements.

- They must manage conflicts of interest (such as between employer and trust) in order to discharge the primary duty to beneficiaries including members.
- They must ensure that they have knowledge and understanding of documents and matters relating to the performance of their functions although they are not expected to be experts.
- They must keep records and accounts.
- They must keep money in a bank account that is separate from that of the employer.
- There are certain disclosure obligations (mainly to members and HMRC).
- They must appoint professional advisors to assist with some of their functions. Professional advisors include an investment advisor, an actuary and an auditor. Professional advisors and certain other people concerned with the running of the scheme are also expected to blow the whistle to the Regulator where there is a breach of a legal duty that would be of material significance to the Regulator.
- Whistleblowers are protected from victimisation by the **Public Interest Disclosure Act 1998**.
- Trustees, administrators and certain other prescribed persons are expected to volunteer information of "notifiable events" to the Regulator when they occur.

Trustees also have a number of powers and discretions.

- They will be given a power to delegate by the trust deed. If there were no such power, the trust could not operate.

- They will have power to amend the scheme with the consent of the employer.
- They will usually have power to augment benefits often after consulting the employer.

Trustees will usually be appointed from the members of the scheme and the majority will be selected by the employer. Since 1997, there has been a requirement for the trustees to have in place a procedure for members to nominate at least one-third of trustees and an appropriate selection procedure if nominations exceed vacancies.

A facility for employers to opt out of the member-nominated procedure was withdrawn by streamlined rules introduced by the **Pensions Act 2004**.

Trustees may also be independent (ie no connection with the employer) and may be professional and/or corporate.

The most important theme behind these rules is that trustees are able to protect current and future interests of members and beneficiaries from interference, benign or otherwise from the employer. Recent legislation has provided further support for trustees in the form of the Pensions Regulator.

The Pensions Acts and Scheme Governance

Pensions used to be regulated by Social Security Acts. This changed with the **Pensions Act 1995**. The Act was a response to well-meaning legislation that suffered from two major drawbacks.

1. It carried few sanctions.
2. It was reactive and, on the whole, unable to intervene until it was too late.

Two features of the 1995 Act were:

(a) almost every obligation or restriction was accompanied by a sanction for non-observance

(b) the Act was pre-emptive by being much more prescriptive of scheme governance and by creating The Occupational Pensions Regulatory Authority (OPRA).

As a first attempt, the 1995 Act was creditable, but had a number of drawbacks. It was therefore superseded by the 2004 Pensions Act (that still incorporated much of the 1995 legislation) which is the main source today.

The main provisions are the creation of the Pensions Regulator, with very wide powers to regulate pension schemes. They include a number of sanctions that may be exercised itself or through the courts. Orders exercised by the Regulator may require an individual or body associated with a scheme to comply with a duty or to desist. Its powers are both preventive and penal.

The main objectives of the Regulator in relation to occupational schemes are to:

- protect the members of work-based schemes (this includes occupational schemes and personal pension and stakeholder schemes operating through a direct payment facility)
- reduce the risk of situations arising which could lead to calls for compensation from the Pension Protection Fund; this requirement, arguably more than any other, has given the Regulator the licence to become very interventionist even to the extent of unpicking funding agreements between employer and trustees
- promote good administration of the schemes it regulates.

The **Pensions Act 2008** introduces new duties on employers in relation to the new framework of personal accounts and auto-enrolment and gives the Pensions Regulator a new objective to maximise compliance with the duties, and ensure safeguards that protect employees are adhered to.

- The requirement for member-nominated trustees. The requirement is for at least one-third to be member-nominated and although there are a number of exemptions, the employer may not opt-out of the requirement. Separate legislation (Employment Rights Act) protects all employee trustees from harassment and victimisation and allows them time off and expenses for conducting trustee business.
- Investment powers allow the trustees significant freedom to invest as if they were absolutely entitled to the assets. However, they must exercise a duty of care and seek proper written advice on the suitability of an investment. They must also have regard to the reason for diversification. In certain circumstances they may delegate their discretion.

Trustees must restrict employer-related investment and are not authorised to make employer loans (except in the case of "small schemes").

The trustees must prepare and maintain a written statement of investment principles that includes a description of the types of investment to be held and the balance between them, the expected investment return and a statement about risk. It must also include a statement of the extent to which social, environmental and ethical considerations are to be taken into account and the policy on voting rights. Investments cannot be excluded (or included) on "ethical grounds" only unless this is permitted in the scheme trust deed.

- The scheme must have implemented an internal dispute resolution procedure. This is a formal process designed to settle disputes or misunderstandings at the place of work rather than allowing them to get out of hand and as far as the Pensions Advisory Service, the Pensions Ombudsman or even the courts.
- The scheme is required to comply with a statutory funding objective (preceded by a minimum funding requirement). This requires the scheme to ensure that the value of assets is adequate to meet its "technical provisions" which are its liabilities.

The statutory funding objective is scheme specific and this meets a criticism of the minimum funding requirement of a "one size fits all" approach. The trustees determine what assumptions should be made. The trustees must seek the agreement of the sponsoring employer before establishing the funding objective and must seek advice from the scheme actuary about assumptions.

The trustees must prepare and maintain a statement of funding principles to ensure that the statutory funding objective is met. This will include a statement of how the objective is to be met and what action will be taken if the objective is missed. The statement must be reviewed every three years.

A Code of Practice published by the Pensions Regulator provides a list of matters that should be covered by actuarial advice and discussed with the employer.

In setting a contribution schedule, the trustees are expected to negotiate robustly with the employer. If the funding objective is not met, the trustees must put in place a recovery plan, a copy of which is sent to the Regulator. The plan must describe how the deficit is to be paid off and in what timeframe. Generally speaking, the Regulator will not accept a recovery period of more than 10 years or which is "back-end loaded". The Regulator will be careful to ensure that the employer and trustees do not reach an agreement which could result in a claim on the Pension Protection Fund.

The employer will be expected to comply with the schedule of contributions and if it does not do so, the contribution becomes a debt on the employer. Unlike the 1995 rules, the legislation does not require non-payment to be referred to the Regulator unless the omission is of material significance. There is a similar provision relating to money purchase schemes.

- There are demanding rules for protecting benefits that have already accrued from being modified. Schemes and employers will wish to change the basis of future accrual from time to time, but past accrual cannot generally be altered unless all the members agree (unlikely). Other backdated modifications can be made if the members agree or the actuary certifies that the change is not materially detrimental to the members.

- There is also a requirement for the employer to consult with employees before making any of a prescribed list of changes to the future accrual under the scheme. This could include increasing retirement age, closing the scheme to new members, closing to future accrual or changing future accrual from defined benefit to defined contribution.

Member Protection when a Scheme Winds Up

The numerous obligations that fall on trustees and employers under the Pensions Acts are designed to ensure that employers deliver their promise to provide a pension benefit described under the rules of the scheme. If you retire from a scheme that has promised a pension of ⅟₆₀th of final salary for each year of service having completed 30 years' service, you must feel confident that you will receive the ³⁰⁄₆₀ths of final salary.

Winding up a pension scheme is a serious option. It may be voluntary or triggered by an event that might suggest, for example, that the scheme is unsustainable.

A voluntary wind-up may be set in motion by the employer after giving notice to the trustees or by the trustees on the advice of the actuary or after the employer has stopped contributing. An involuntary wind-up may be caused by an employer going into liquidation or receivership.

It may appear to be an easy option when trading conditions are difficult to stop contributions or wind up a defined benefit scheme, but this is not the case.

- There is an obligation on employers to make good a funding deficiency on the winding up of the scheme. The debt is not a preferential debt so will rank behind the banks who are likely to have priority.

- The value of members' benefits is calculated on a "discontinuance basis".

The discontinuance basis assumes that there are sufficient assets to provide the full value of the accrued pension immediately and by way of an annuity. This contrasts with the ongoing basis of valuation that allows for future investment returns (the "discount rate") and targets the appropriate benefit at retirement. By way of example, a scheme that is fully funded on an ongoing basis may only be 60–70% funded on a discontinuance basis.

There are other options open to the employer and trustees.

- The scheme can be closed to new members and/or future accrual. This will not yield an immediate saving because existing accrual must be honoured.
- The scheme may be bought out (transferred) to a specialist trustee company or a life assurance company. This would assume no further accrual or new members. The transfer value of a "bulk transfer" will be supplemented by a premium (because the transferee can expect no further funding from the employer) which will mean that this is an expensive option in terms of cash flow, but removes future liability for the employer.
- The trustees may purchase annuities to be held as assets of the scheme. Again this is not immediately a cheap option, but allows the trustees to "contract out" some of the fund management to a life assurance company. This is known as a "buy-in".

If an employer becomes insolvent and the scheme is in deficit, the Pension Protection Fund may intervene in order to ensure a minimum level of pension is available to members.

In the event of a wind-up, the trustees will "buy out" their liability by way of immediate and deferred annuities. Members are given an option to transfer to an alternative contract. Annuities tend to be quite expensive which again increases the cost of the buy-out.

If the wind-up reveals a deficit, the trustees will first try to recover the shortfall from the employer. If the employer is unable to make up the shortfall, perhaps because it is insolvent and other creditors rank higher, there is a priority order for meeting the claims of different classes of member. This priority order has changed on a number of occasions and the last change was prompted by the introduction of the Pension Protection Fund (PPF). To give an idea of how the priority order works, we can look at the current order:

(a) benefits available from certain insurance contracts

(b) any other liability for benefits to the extent of what would otherwise be provided by the Pension Protection Fund (this includes the full value of benefits for anyone who has passed retirement date)

(c) any benefits derived from additional voluntary contributions

(d) any other liability for benefits.

A feature of this list is that all liabilities must be met under one heading before moving to the next. So, if after meeting the liability for benefits under a, b and c there is little or nothing left for d, then members will lose entitlement under d. The value of liabilities is not proportionately spread over all classes.

Under the rules in force before 2005 and before the PPF, there would often be very little remaining after accounting for pensions in payment leaving the deferred pensioners with little or nothing.

If the PPF concludes that there is a funding shortfall that cannot be made up by an employer and there is no practical prospect of a corporate rescue, the PPF will take over the scheme. It will ensure that members receive a minimum benefit. The PPF is funded partly by the assets it acquires from failed schemes and partly by a levy on viable schemes. The levy comprises an administration levy and a risk-based levy (based partly on the strength of the employer).

The PPF pays 100% of pension entitlement for members who have reached normal pension age and 90% for other members. The pension available to other members is also subject to an indexed and age-related "cap" that is £33,219.36 (the 100% figure) for a 65-year-old in 2011/12.

Example

Matthew is 63 and a member of a defined benefit scheme under which the normal pension age is 65. He has an accrued pension of £50,000. His employer becomes insolvent and cannot be rescued. The scheme is only 60% funded on a discontinuance basis although it had been valued at 95% of liabilities on an ongoing basis in the previous year.

Matthew must expect that his pension will be paid by the Pension Protection Fund and that his pension will probably be less than £30,000 a year (90% of the accrued pension and subject to the cap).

> **Example**
> Tom is in the same scheme, but his accrued pension is only £10,000. He is 55. His PPF pension will be 90% of £10,000 (£9000), but the cap will not apply.

The PPF has no application to defined contribution schemes. The value of benefits is the value of the account or policy which can only be reduced in value by a fall in the value of assets and the impact of charges.

A controversial feature of the PPF is that successive governments since 2005 have refused to guarantee its benefits, although it would be very difficult for a government to let PPF fail.

Key Facts

- Pension scheme members are now protected by trust law, financial services regulation and the pensions Acts.
- Trusts are a peculiarly British legal concept that separates the legal ownership of property from the right to enjoy the use of that property or the income from it. Trusts offer security and qualify the scheme for tax relief.
- Two features of the 1995 Act were:
  - almost every obligation or restriction was accompanied by a sanction for non-observance
  - the Act was pre-emptive by being much more prescriptive of scheme governance and by creating The Occupational Pensions Regulatory Authority (OPRA).
- The 2004 Pensions Act created the Pensions Regulator.
- A defined benefit scheme is required to comply with a statutory funding objective (preceded by a minimum funding requirement). This requires the scheme to ensure that the value of assets is adequate to meet its "technical provisions" which are its liabilities.
- If the funding objective is not met, the trustees must put in place a recovery plan, a copy of which is sent to the Regulator. The plan must describe how the deficit is to be paid off and in what timeframe.
- It is not an easy option to stop contributions to a defined benefit scheme when trading conditions are difficult.
- If a sponsoring employer becomes insolvent and the scheme is underfunded, the scheme may be taken over by the Pension Protection Fund.

• Benefits from the PPF are reduced and capped if the member has not reached normal pension age when the insolvency arises.

QUESTIONS AND ANSWERS

Q1   In relation to occupational schemes, what are the primary responsibilities of the DWP?

A   • Supervising contracting-out
• Member protection legislation.

Q2   What are the main functions of pension trustees?

A   In the context of pension schemes, the trustees are required to:
• collect and invest contributions and other input
• manage the investments by balancing the twin objectives of maximising the return and protecting the capital
• pay the right benefit (in accordance with the scheme trust deed and rules) to the right members or beneficiaries at the right time.

They also have a number of statutory duties, including accounting for tax.

Q3   A trustee must always act with utmost good faith. How does he or she go about this?

A   Be impartial at all times and bear in mind that the duty is solely to the members and beneficiaries of the scheme.

Remember that he or she is not a representative of anybody and his or her personal opinions are of no consequence in determining the appropriate actions that he or she is required to perform for the beneficiaries.

Perform his or her duties diligently and act as a prudent person of business, using common sense and relying upon expert, professional advice as and when necessary in order to assist him or her in reaching a proper conclusion.

Q4   What is the member-nominated trustee requirement of occupational schemes.

A   The requirement is for at least one-third to be member-nominated and although there are a number of exemptions.

Q5   What are the statutory objectives of the Pensions Regulator?

A   To protect the benefits of members of work-based schemes (this includes occupational schemes and personal pension and stakeholder schemes operating through a direct payment facility).
    To reduce the risk of situations arising which could lead to calls for compensation from the Pension Protection Fund and to promote good administration of the schemes it regulates.

Q6   In summary, what benefit does the Pension Protection Fund pay to members?

A   The PPF pays 100% of pension entitlement for members who have reached normal pension age and 90% for other members.

Q7   Why is the PPF not guaranteed?

A   A controversial feature of the PPF is that successive governments since 2005 have refused to guarantee its benefits, although it would be very difficult for a government to let PPF fail.

CHAPTER 8

Transfer of Accrued Benefits

General Right to Transfer

The member who has accrued benefits under a registered pension scheme may generally transfer those accrued benefits (crystallised or uncrystallised) to another registered scheme without fiscal penalty. HMRC rules are designed to ensure that on the one hand, members' pensions are suitably "portable" to reflect their circumstances and wishes, but on the other hand, transfers do not become a vehicle for avoiding tax and the restrictions imposed by the tax rules.

If the transfer takes place between registered schemes, the only significant tax restrictions relate to benefits accrued before 6 April 2006 where protection is claimed against the lifetime allowance for funds that were already significant at that date (enhanced protection) or where the member is able to protect a lump sum that exceeds 25% of benefits or a pension age that is lower than 55 under the "transitional protection rules".

The tax rules will always be uppermost in the member's mind because if they are not followed, the transfer may represent an unauthorised payment and be taxed accordingly.

However, there are other considerations that are fairly basic and will vary according to whether the transfer involves a defined benefit or money purchase scheme.

It is worth noting here that transfers in this context refer to transfers of preserved pensions where a member has left scheme service rather than "opting out" of a scheme which will rarely be to the member's advantage, especially if the scheme was proving defined benefits and/or providing related death benefits.

Financial advisors are now heavily regulated when giving advice on transfers and this section may help to explain why.

The Right to Transfer

The member who leaves an occupational scheme having completed two years' service usually has a right to a transfer value. The right is to transfer to any occupational pension scheme or to a deferred annuity or an approved or provisionally approved personal pension scheme.

There is no obligation upon either scheme trustees or an insurance company to accept a transfer value except that a registered stakeholder pension scheme cannot refuse to accept a transfer value from a registered pension scheme.

The member loses his or her right to transfer on or after what is known as the last option date. This is the later of one year before normal retirement age and six months after the date when his pensionable service terminates. Furthermore, the right to take a transfer value must be exercised by written application to the trustees or managers of the scheme.

Money Purchase to Money Purchase Transfers

In essence, the member anticipates a benefit that is entirely dependent on the net investment return on scheme investments and the pension that the emerging fund is able to purchase. The decision to transfer will simply substitute another fund which is unlikely to offer any greater security of outcome. Its attraction may be the investment options it can offer.

Very important in the decision-making process will be the incidence and amount of charges, whether they are initial charges on the new plan, ongoing charges on the fund or exit charges on early encashment or transfer.

The advisor will provide a comparison projection of benefits and a rate of return required to match the benefits on the original plan, but this is only a projection designed to disclose the effect of charges: it is neither a guarantee nor a promise. The future return is dependent on the skills of the investment manager and the investment performance (unknown) less the impact of charges (fairly well-known).

84

Defined Benefit to Money Purchase Transfers

This is in many senses a much more complex decision. There is rarely a general right or wrong answer, and the advice and decision will be based on what is most suitable for a particular member: there is no "one size fits all". The decision is rendered difficult by the comparison of qualitative factors as well as those of amounts. They involve attitudes to risk as well as projected benefits. So, it is important to grasp some fundamental concepts (that appear very obvious when taken out of context).

The promise

Defined benefit schemes offer a promise of future benefits. This is not the same as a guarantee because the promise can only be as strong as the employer's facility to fund it and as a back-stop, for the compensation schemes to make good any shortfall. The employer is under legal pressure to ensure that defined benefit schemes are adequately funded, but may become insolvent and incapable of delivering on the promise. If the scheme then becomes underfunded, the Pension Protection Fund may become involved, but compensation is capped and the Government has refused to guarantee the future of the Fund.

In fact, it is extremely unlikely that a government could withdraw or reduce PPF compensation, but that is the type of risk that must be appreciated. Capping the compensation for a relatively young member means that the promise is only as good as the employer's ability to pay in respect of a pension above the PPF cap.

The guarantee

From this it can be deduced that there are no guarantees in respect of the defined benefit scheme, the PPF or indeed, the transfer vehicle. There are simply degrees of risk.

Transfer Plans

Although the transfer rules allow transfers between all registered schemes, the most common use of the facility is to transfer accrued rights to an individual plan. There are two options:

Personal pension plan

The application is made by the member and the cash equivalent transfer value is allocated to arrangements within the personal pension scheme. Transfer may be from a money purchase scheme or a defined benefit scheme and the objective may be to provide greater retirement flexibility or control over investments. Advice to transfer from a defined benefit scheme must be accompanied by a thorough analysis of the options including a "critical yield analysis" which calculates the rate of return required to match what would otherwise have been available from an occupational scheme.

Trustees of a scheme cannot make transfers to a personal pension scheme without the member's application.

"Buy-out" policy (s.32 policy)

This option offers transfer to an annuity and may allow trustees to buy out their liability to provide benefits by transferring funds to a life assurance company. The annuity may provide benefits immediately or may provide deferred benefits.

Transfers to buy-out policies may only be made from defined benefit occupational schemes and contracted-out money purchase occupational schemes (and other buy out policies).

Buy-out annuities are offered by trustees to members when the scheme is to be wound up. They are not usually good value and the wind up process will invite members to select their transfer plan and offer the buy-out policy as a "default" option if a selection is not made before a published deadline.

Transfer to an individual policy must be approached with caution because it can prompt a loss of transitional protection and in particular scheme specific lump sum protection. The requirements of a block transfer preclude the use of "buy-out" policies as each policy is regarded by legislation as an individual scheme.

Key Facts

- Members of occupational pension schemes have a right to transfer accrued benefits before the "last option date".
- Transfers from defined benefit to money purchase schemes involve considerations of promises against projected benefits and the strength of the employer covenant.

- A buy-out plan allows the trustees to buy out their liability to provide benefits, for example when a scheme is wound up.
- Advice to transfer must be accompanied by a thorough analysis including a critical yield analysis.
- A transfer may prompt a loss of transitional protection.

QUESTIONS AND ANSWERS

Q1 **Why must a member have regard to the tax rules when transferring benefits?**

A   The tax rules will always be uppermost in the member's mind because if they are not followed, the transfer may represent an unauthorised payment and be taxed accordingly.

   Transfer to an individual policy must be approached with caution because it can prompt a loss of transitional protection and in particular scheme specific lump sum protection.

Q2 **What is the obligation on a pension scheme to accept a transfer from another scheme?**

A   There is no obligation upon either scheme trustees or an insurance company to accept a transfer value except that a registered stakeholder pension scheme cannot refuse to accept a transfer value from a registered pension scheme.

Q3 **When does a member lose the right to transfer?**

A   The member loses the right to transfer on or after what is known as the last option date. This is the later of one year before normal retirement age and six months after the date when his pensionable service terminates.

Q4 **Why is it inaccurate to describe defined benefits as guaranteed?**

A   Defined benefit schemes offer a promise of future benefits. This is not the same as a guarantee because the promise can only be as strong as the employer's facility to fund it and as a back-stop, for the compensation schemes to make good any shortfall.

CHAPTER 9

The State Scheme and Contracting-out

Key Features

The framework of tax reliefs available to private pensions supplements a well-established State scheme. Features of the State pension scheme are as follows.

- It is contributory and not means tested. Qualification for benefit is based on the individual's National Insurance contribution record rather than his or her other financial resources.
- The scheme comprises a flat-rate basic State pension that is available to those who have been self-employed or employees and an additional earnings-related pension that is available to those who have been employees.
- Registered pension schemes or their members have an option to contract out of the earnings-related component. They pay lower National Insurance contributions (reduced by the "rebate") on the basis that the scheme will provide an alternative benefit.
- The State pension credit is not part of the State scheme. It is not contributory and is means-tested as an extension of income support benefit. It is available from State pension age.
- The State scheme has changed over the years (mainly in 1978, 1988 and 2002) and individuals retain benefits accrued in previous years. In the 2012 Budget, the Government proposed that in the next Parliament it would legislate to introduce a universal pension. The

universal pension would be payable at a flat-rate (£140 a week in 2012 terms) and would replace the basic state pension, the additional pension and the pension credit.

State Pension Age

Until the tax year 2009/10, the State pension age was 60 for women and 65 for men. In recognition of the equal aspirations of men and women and the improved life expectancy of contributors, recent legislation has taken steps to equalise and increase these ages. Between 2010 and 2018, the State pension age for women is scheduled to increase to 65.

Between 2018 and 2020, the State pension age will increase to 66 for men and women.

The state pension age is scheduled to increase to 67 between 2026 and 2028 and between 2044 and 2046 (with a view to increasing to 68). In the 2012 Budget, the Government announced that the state pension age would be linked to average life expectancy at some stage in the future.

An individual's State pension age is determined by his or her date of birth.

The current rules allow the individual to postpone the State pension. It will then be increased by 1/5th of 1% for each week the pension is postponed beyond State pension age. Alternatively, after a postponement of one year, the individual can take a taxable lump sum instead of the increases.

The State pension may never be taken earlier than State pension age, but the individual may have access to a range of other State benefits.

Inflation-proofing

From 2011, the increase to the basic State pension is based on the greater of the increase in national average earnings, the increase in the RPI and the increase in the Consumer Prices Index subject to a minimum 2.5%. The additional pension will increase with the Consumer Prices Index (CPI).

The CPI excludes housing costs and has consistently risen at a slower rate than the RPI. Earnings increase faster than both indices as a general rule.

References to "inflation-proofing" should be read with caution. The protection cannot be absolute, if only because we all have different expenditure priorities, but it is generally accepted that inflation for pensioners is much higher that that demonstrated by the main indices (RPI and CPI) because of the greater emphasis on spending necessities such as food and heating which form a large proportion of the pensioner's spending.

Basic State Pension — Qualification

Not everybody qualifies for the full basic State pension. Until the 2009/10 tax year, the full rate of pension was only available to the self-employed and employees whose NI contribution record was complete for at least 90% of their working life (a working life was 49 years for a man and 44 years for a woman). National Insurance is payable when employee earnings in a week are at least the primary threshold (employees) and the year counts for qualification purposes if the threshold is reached in at least 50 out of 52 weeks of the year. There is a minimum earnings requirement for a year to count in respect of the self-employed.

This was a tough qualification standard that was mitigated by a framework of contribution credits and home responsibility protection that reduced the qualification for individuals who were detained at home by caring or parenting obligations. The system was widely regarded as unfair on many women who almost necessarily could expect interrupted careers. So, from 2010/11, the qualification period is reduced to 30 years for both men and women.

Additional Pension

The additional pension has changed over the years. This remains important because an individual who retires today will retain benefits that have accrued under each regime. There are three main additional pensions, but each is only available to those who have been employees.

The graduated pension was only available in respect of employment between 1961 and 1975 and is insignificant compared with its successors.

The State earnings-related pension (SERPS) was introduced in 1978 and remains the basis of the State second pension (S2P) that was introduced in 2002.

The original SERPS aimed to provide a maximum pension of 25% of "band earnings" (see below) over a working life. If contributions were not paid or credited for some of that working life, the SERPS pension would be proportionately reduced.

The 25% maximum benefit was subsequently reduced to 20% in stages from 2001/2002, but only in respect of future accrual. So, for example, anyone who retired in 2015 would receive a pension made up of pre-2001 accrual and post-2000 accrual.

The relevant percentage is applied to the average of revalued earnings that fall between the lower and upper earnings limits over a full working life. Each year's "band earnings" is revalued in line with the average earnings index and this ensures that the benefit enjoys a measure of inflation-proofing. When it is paid, the pension increases with the Consumer Prices Index.

In 2002, SERPS underwent a major change that was designed to benefit the lower paid. The band of earnings between the lower and upper earnings limits was split into three bands. The contributor retained benefits accrued prior to 2002.

On the lowest band of earnings, the rate of accrual was based on 40% (20% prior to 2002). Anyone with earnings of at least the lower earnings limit is assumed to be earnings at least the full lower rate band. On the middle band, the accrual rate was based on 10% (20% prior to 2002) and on the upper band, the accrual was based on 20% (20%). For any contributor whose earnings fell into the upper band (or higher) the average accrual rate would be 20% and the contributor's "band earnings".

From 2009, the earnings-related pension is calculated by reference to earnings between the lower earnings limit and an upper accrual point (UAP). The UAP will remain fixed. From 2010, the upper accrual band is abolished so benefits will accrue at 40% and 10%. By about 2030, the effect of freezing the UAP, but continuing to increase the other thresholds will mean that the additional pension will become a flat rate benefit. In the 2012 Budget, the Government announced that it would legislate for a universal flat-rate pension in the next Parliament. This would replace the basic state pension, the additional pension and the pension credit.

State Pension Credit

The State pension credit is an extension of income support to individuals who have reached State pension age. It is non-contributory, but means-tested. The problem with this type of benefit is that the means testing can unfairly penalise those who have put money aside in private pension plans. The benefit therefore has a complicated way of boosting the benefit where there is evidence of pension savings. So, there are three categories of potential claimant.

1. Those whose income is less than the basic State pension. They are entitled to a minimum guarantee credit that ensures the claimant receives the amount of the basic State pension.
2. Those who have income between the basic State pension and a threshold just above that amount. For these individuals, their benefit will be supplemented by an additional amount (the savings credit) of up to £18.54 (2012/13) for a single person subject to this amount being cut back the higher the individual's income from other sources.
3. Those whose income is above a higher threshold and no pension credit is available.

Contracting-out

Contracting-out is a facility that allows employers or employees to elect to pay lower rates of National Insurance providing a private arrangement meets the special requirements of a contracted-out scheme.

Contracting-out of SERPS was originally (1978) an option only available to occupational schemes in respect of all their members. The obligation on the scheme was to provide a pension at State pension age of at least the guaranteed minimum pension (GMP). The GMP was roughly equal to the amount of SERPS foregone, but where it fell short of the SERPS, the difference was, to an extent, paid by the State scheme.

In 1997, this basis of contracting-out was replaced by a reference scheme test. Instead of requiring the scheme to provide a GMP, it had to exhibit certain features in respect of its benefit structure. The reference scheme was a model theoretical scheme based on a pension benefit of ⅛₀th of final pensionable pay for each year of service.

Reference Scheme Test (RST)

Satisfaction of the RST must be certified by an actuary, usually the actuary appointed to the scheme.

The minimum requirements of the reference scheme are:

- ⅛₀th accrual rate
- qualifying earnings are 90% of the employee's "banded earnings" in that year
- pension is payable from a normal retirement date of 65 (lower normal retirement dates are permissible, provided the pension scheme benefits are equivalent to those available under the reference scheme benchmark)
- provide a widow(er)'s pension of at least 50% of the member's pension.

Annual pension enhancement for benefits accumulated after 6 April 1997 would be at least statutory revaluation.

An important feature of the 1997 changes was that members retained benefit rights accrued prior to April 1997 and this means that many individuals retain rights to GMP.

Contracting-out options were extended in 1988 in two ways.

1. In addition to the defined benefit basis of contracting-out (GMP basis), employers were given the option of contracting out members of money purchase schemes that met the requirements of a contracted-out money purchase scheme (COMPS). The money purchase basis simply required the employer to make a minimum payment to the scheme and the National Insurance contributions of employer and member were correspondingly reduced. The employer was able to recover a contribution from the member. The requirement of the scheme was to ensure that "minimum payments" were ring-fenced to provide a protected rights pension. Protected rights were in no way guaranteed, but the benefit was required to meet certain criteria: originally not available until State pension age, pension provided by an annuity calculated on a unisex basis, no lump sum, statutory inflation linking. In 2012, protected rights will be abolished

2. The second basis of contracting out was also on a money purchase basis, but was available to individuals who were able to contract out by way of a personal pension plan. It was abolished in 2012. Again, the benefit took the form of protected rights. However, the required contribution was deducted from the National Insurance contribution by (latterly) HMRC and redirected directly to the plan after the end of the tax year. The member paid the same rate of National Insurance whether or not contracted out on this basis.

Key Facts

- The State scheme is contributory and not means tested. Qualification for benefit is based on the individual's National Insurance contribution record rather than his or her other financial resources.
- The scheme comprises a flat-rate basic State pension that is available to those who have been self-employed or employees and an additional earnings-related pension that is available to those who have been employees.
- Registered pension schemes or their members have an option to contract-out of the earnings-related component. They pay lower National Insurance contributions (reduced by the "rebate") on the basis that the scheme will provide an alternative benefit.
- A defined benefit scheme may contract-out on a reference scheme basis
- The State pension credit is not part of the State scheme. It is not contributory and is means-tested as an extension of income support benefit. It is available from State pension age.
- The State scheme has changed over the years (mainly in 1978, 1988 and 2002) and individuals retain benefits accrued in previous years.

QUESTIONS AND ANSWERS

Q1 Why is the option to contract-out not available to the self-employed?

A The self-employed only qualify for the basic State pension and contracting-out is an option in respect of the additional pension.

Q2 Why is qualification for the State pension fundamentally different from qualification for the State pension credit?

A The State pension is contributory — qualification is based on NI contributions paid. The State pension credit is non-contributory, but means-tested.

Q3 Against what index is it proposed that the basic State pension will increase in 2014?

A The earnings index (or CPI if greater).

Q4 Against what index will SERPS be increased in 2014?

A   The CPI.

Q5   What is the contribution qualification period for the maximum basic State pension from 2010/2011?

A   30 years.

Q6   In general terms, what is function of the upper accrual point?

A   It is the limit on earnings against which the additional pension is calculated.

Q7   How does contracting-out work in respect of pre-1997 DB rights?

A   Employer and employee pay lower rates of NI (reduced by'the rebate') and the member benefits under a reference scheme.

Q8   How did this change in 1997?

A   Before April 1997, the scheme had to provide a guaranteed minimum pension.

CHAPTER 10

Death Benefits

Importance of Death Benefits

Death benefits are an important feature of retirement planning. They are integral to commercial products whether they are individual plans or employer sponsored group arrangements and also to the state scheme. They are recognised by the tax and benefit system.

At the same time, there is a concern of Government that death benefits should not be used to support tax-efficient estate planning so there will always be a tension between the objectives of supporting the bereaved family and estate tax leakage. To quote a DWP spokesman during the 2004–2006 pension tax reforms, "a pension is a pension is a pension". The implication here was that a pension is an income for life (or the lives of the member and dependants) and not intended primarily to create wealth for succeeding generations.

Death benefits may be provided in the form of a lump sum or an income, but more commonly in private arrangements, by a combination of both.

The death benefit options will differ according to whether the member has taken retirement benefits ("crystallised") or not ("uncrystallised" — remember, you need not have retired from work to take the retirement.

Death before Age 75 — Lump Sum Tax Rules

Life assurance

The return of fund under a money purchase scheme may be supplemented by a term assurance contract.

As a general rule, no tax relief is available for contributions to a personal life assurance policy (a "non-group life" policy). This differs from earlier rules.

Tax relief may be available in respect of personal life assurance policies that are protected policies. Protected policies are policies that were established before a date in 2007 and which have not been significantly varied since.

Income benefits

In the event of death before benefits have crystallised as retirement benefits, legislation allows the fund to provide a dependant's pension. Whereas the lump sum may be tax-free, the dependant's pension is taxed as income in the hands of the beneficiary. However, payment of a dependant's pension will never constitute a benefit crystallisation event and there will never be a liability for the lifetime allowance charge.

A dependant's pension is only available to a dependant as defined by the scheme rules and within the legislative definition.

Authorised Lump Sum Death Benefits

Lump sum death benefits that meet the requirement of the lump sum death benefit rule are treated as authorised payments. There is only one lump sum death benefit rule which lists the circumstances when a lump sum can be paid following the death of the member. A death benefit lump sum paid before age 75 in respect of previously uncrystallised benefits counts towards the member's lifetime allowance and the personal representatives are responsible for any lifetime allowance charge payable. Lump sum death benefits paid after age 74 are subject to tax at 55%, but there is no liability to inheritance tax.

Defined benefits scheme lump sum

The defined benefits scheme lump sum is payable on the death of the member at any age and triggers a test against the lifetime allowance. It is tax-free to the extent that the lifetime allowance if it is before age 75 is not exceeded in respect of the member (when the excess is subject to the lifetime allowance charge). It must be paid within two years of the member's death to be a defined benefits lump sum death benefit (and therefore an "authorised payment" not subject to penal rates of tax).

Lump sum death benefits paid after age 74 are subject to tax at 55% from 6 April 2011. Some lump sums (in respect of benefits that have already been crystallised as "retirement benefits") are taxable before age 75 at 55%.

A defined benefit lump sum is not necessarily a lump sum linked to a defined benefit pension arrangement: it refers to a death benefit calculated by reference to a multiple of earnings, service or another factor linked to employment. It may even be expressed as a fixed amount if this is expressed as a benefit and there is no option to choose how the amount should be applied at date of death (eg pension or lump sum). If it is merely a sum assured it is a money purchase arrangement and this may be significant if the member has claimed transitional protection.

Group Life Assurance and Personal Pension Schemes

It has long been common for employers to include members of an occupational scheme in a group life assurance arrangement in order to provide lump sum and income death benefits (under a defined benefit scheme, there are no individual funds for members). The arrangements are written subject to the trust and enjoy tax benefits on contributions and benefits (contributions are tax-free as are lump sum benefits as part of a registered pension scheme).

Individuals are entitled to be members of the life assurance section by virtue of death benefits being associated with the normal activities of an occupational pension scheme. However, if the employee does not qualify for benefits under the pension section (perhaps newer employees are members of a group personal pension scheme), they may not be members of the registered group life scheme. There are alternatives such as an "excepted group life policy" that, in effect, enjoys similar reliefs from tax.

Pension protection lump sum death benefit

A pension protection lump sum death benefit is payable where the pension is in payment and the member has specified that it should be treated as a pension protection lump sum benefit. In the case of a pension scheme, the amount is limited to the initial pension multiplied by the relevant valuation factor (20) from which is deducted payments already made by way of pension and previous pension protection lump sums. It is similar to the commuted guarantee applicable to occupational schemes prior to 6 April 2006. The lump sum is subject to income tax at 55% which is chargeable on the scheme administrator, but deductible from the payment.

Uncrystallised funds lump sum death benefit

An uncrystallised funds lump sum death benefit is payable in respect of money purchase schemes and is tax-free within the lifetime allowance. The lump sum must be paid within two years of the member's death or within two years of when the scheme administrator could reasonably be expected to have known of it first. It is paid in respect of uncrystallised funds (ie not applied to the provision of retirement benefits). The permitted maximum is the value of the member's money purchase funds. This may be supplemented by life assurance.

Uncrystallised lump sums are subject to income tax at 55% if death occurs after the member has reached age 75.

Annuity protection lump sum death benefit

The annuity protection lump sum death benefit mirrors the similar benefit for defined benefit schemes (pension protection lump sum). It is payable where the member had started taking a scheme pension or lifetime annuity. The annuity protection limit is the amount crystallised (eg the annuity purchase price) less instalments of pension paid and less annuity protection lump sum death benefits already paid. The lump sum is subject to income tax at 55% which is chargeable on the scheme administrator, but deductible from the payment.

Drawdown lump sum death benefit

The drawdown lump sum death benefit is payable where the member was taking benefits by way of income drawdown. It is also available where a dependant was taking benefits by way of income drawdown and died.

The permitted maximum is the value of the funds designated to provide the income drawdown, at the time of the claim. The lump sum is subject to income tax at 55% which is chargeable on the administrator, but may be deducted from the payment.

Note: It is possible to have uncrystallised and drawdown funds in the same arrangement and each part will be treated differently for tax purposes on death.

There are alternatives to paying a lump sum that are less frequently used. The fund may be used to provide a dependant's pension. The pension may be:
- a dependant's drawdown pension
- a dependant's secure pension such as an annuity.

The drawdown pension will continue for life.

Charity lump sum death benefit

A charity lump sum death benefit is payable in the event of the death of a member or dependant who is taking benefits by way of drawdown. There must be no surviving dependants of the member. The lump sum is payable to a charity nominated by the member/dependant.

The permitted maximum is the value of drawdown pension rights immediately before the payment is made. The payment is tax-free if made to a charity.

A charity lump sum may also be paid from uncrystallised funds on the death of a member if there are no surviving dependants.

Trivial commutation lump sum death benefit

A trivial commutation lump sum death benefit is payable to a dependant entitled under the scheme when the value of the fund under the scheme does not exceed £18,000. No further benefits are then payable to the dependant in respect of the member. A trivial commutation lump sum is taxed as income in the hands of the dependant.

Trivial lump sums are to be excluded when an individual's claim for certain State benefits is means-tested. Those benefits are housing benefit, council tax benefit and pension credit where the individual is over 60.

Winding-up lump sum death benefit

A winding-up lump sum death benefit is similar to the trivial payment and is payable to a dependant entitled under the scheme where the scheme is being wound up and the amount does not exceed £18,000. There is no age restriction. No further benefits are then payable to the dependant in respect of the member. The lump sum is taxed as income in the hands of the dependant.

An anti-avoidance measure requires that the winding-up is not being undertaken primarily to pay a lump sum and the fine for contravening this requirement is £3000 payable by the administrator in respect of each individual to whom the lump sum was paid.

Life cover lump sum (funeral expenses, etc)

This is only payable if the member was over 75 at date of death and in respect of a pre-6 April 2006 approved occupational scheme that allowed payment of small lump sums for funeral expenses or grants.

Authorised Income Death Benefits

The benefits payable on death after retirement benefits have been taken will depend to an extent on what options the member chose at retirement.

Annuity

When an individual purchases an annuity with a pension fund, he or she will be offered a range of benefit options to suit personal circumstances. Each of the options is likely to have a cost that will be reflected in the annuity rate — the income purchase with the lump sum. Options include inflation protection (index linking) and a choice of payment frequencies. They will also include three main death benefits.
1. A dependant's pension.
2. A guaranteed payment period (maximum 10 years).
3. An annuity protection lump sum.

Dependant's pension

This ensures that on the death of the member, the pension will continue for the life of a named dependant. The pension will be taxed at the dependant's rate of income tax. Adding a dependant to the annuity (when it is purchased) will usually reduce the rate of income. The market place takes a narrower view of who can be a dependant than the tax rules. It will usually be a spouse or registered civil partner.

Guaranteed payment period

The guaranteed payment period is a provision that requires the annuity to pay for a minimum term (term certain) whether or not it is survived by the member. So if there is a 10-year guarantee and the member dies at the end of year seven, the payments will continue for another three years. The payments are subject to income tax based on the recipient's tax status, but will usually also form part of the member's estate for inheritance tax purposes so they are not very tax efficient. Guarantee payments are not allowed on dependants' pensions under the tax rules. **Note:** That guarantee payments are not restricted to dependants.

Who is a dependant?

A person who was married to the member at the date of the member's death is a dependant, as can be a member of a relationship registered under the **Civil Partnership Act 2004**. The scheme rules may provide that an individual who was married to the member when the member's pension started shall be treated as a dependant even though the couple may have subsequently divorced.

A child of the member (including adopted) is a dependant of the member if he or she has not reached age 23 or having reached that age remains dependent on the member in the opinion of the scheme administrator because of physical or mental impairment. If the dependant's pension was in payment at 6 April 2006 or the member's pension was in payment at that date, the benefit will be payable to the later age of 23 and the end of full-time educational or vocational training.

Any other individual may be a dependant if, in the opinion of the scheme administrator, he or she was at the date of the member's death:
• financially dependent on the member
• financially interdependent, or
• dependent on the member because of physical or mental impairment.
A child cannot be a dependant beyond age 22 solely because he or she remains financially dependent or in full-time education or training, except if he or she enjoys transitional protection.

Payments may be made to children aged 23 or over in certain prescribed circumstances where they are in full-time education or vocational training. These cover pre-2006 pensions.

Dependants' pensions are available to children over the age of 22 who are financially dependent if they were in payment before July 2008.

State Scheme

The surviving spouse or civil partner is entitled to the following.

1. A tax-free lump sum bereavement payment (£2000) providing he or she is not living with another individual of the opposite sex as man and wife. A person is entitled to a bereavement payment if:

   (a) either that person was under State pension age at the time the spouse/civil partner died or the spouse/civil partner was then not entitled to a Category A State retirement pension (Category A pension is a pension in respect of the individual's own National Insurance contributions); and

   (b) the spouse/civil partner had actually paid NICs on earnings of at least 25 times the weekly National Insurance LEL in any given tax year before he or she had died. (The equivalent number of Class 2 (self-employed) NICs or Class 3 (voluntary) NICs is also sufficient to meet the entitlement condition).

2. A taxable bereavement allowance if the spouse or civil partner is over 45, but has not yet reached State pension age and providing he or she is not living with another individual of the opposite sex as man and wife.

3. A taxable widowed parent's allowance, subject to the same conditions described above.

4. If the surviving spouse has reached 65, then he or she may inherit the full basic rate pension and between 50% and 100% of SERPS/S2P (see below). This is the "Category B" retirement pension. The allowance is not payable if a widow is claiming a retirement pension.

The bereavement allowance is payable in similar circumstances to the previous widow's pension. The surviving spouse or civil partner must be aged 45 or over and the allowance is reduced by 7% for each year by which the age at the time of the husband's death falls short of 55. The maximum benefit is dependent on the deceased spouse having sufficient qualifying years (90% of the working life for a full pension). The qualifying years did not reduce in 2010 when the threshold reduced for the basic retirement pension. It is only payable for 52 weeks or until earlier remarriage.

The widowed parent's allowance is payable until the youngest child is 16 or 19 if at school. It comprises a basic allowance plus an earnings related addition.

Widowed parent's allowance is payable to a person whose spouse/civil partner died on or after 7 April 2001, provided he or she was under State pension age at the date of the spouse's death.

It is also payable to a man whose wife died before 9 April 2001, provided that he has not remarried and was under State pension age at that date.

A contribution record of 90% of the working life remains in determining eligibility for full widowed parent's allowance.

The surviving spouse or civil partner is entitled to widowed parent's allowance if he or she is entitled to child benefit in respect of a child who is a son or daughter of the surviving spouse or civil partner and the deceased spouse or civil partner, or in respect of a child for whom the deceased spouse or civil partner was immediately before his or her death entitled to child benefit or, if the surviving spouse/civil partner and the deceased spouse or civil partner were residing together immediately before his or her death, in respect of a child for whom the surviving spouse or civil partner was then entitled to child benefit.

Widowed parent's allowance will continue while the above conditions are met, provided that the surviving spouse does not remarry or the surviving civil partner does not enter into a new civil partnership. If the surviving spouse does remarry or the surviving civil partner does enter into a new civil partnership, then entitlement is lost. Even if the surviving spouse or civil partner still has dependent children, the widowed parent's allowance will cease when the claimant reaches State pension age. The claimant would then move to State retirement pension.

Widowed parent's allowance is fully taxable.

When a widow or widower reaches 65 then the Category B (claimed in respect of a spouse's National Insurance contributions) pension becomes payable. This comprises the inherited basic State pension and a proportion of the additional (eg S2P) pension as if they had been receiving the bereavement or widowed parent's allowance continuously. For these purposes, it is assumed that bereavement allowance included an additional pension (S2P) as under the old widow's pension. Where a widow or widower has become entitled twice or more to a Category B pension, the individual may choose which is more favourable, or in the absence of making a choice, will be given the higher pension.

Note: That the Category B pension is not available if the claimant has remarried. Also a claimant spouse may top up an inherited entitlement with his or her own contributions where it falls short of the possible maximum.

Inherited Second Pension

If an individual dies while receiving a State earnings-related pension, the individual's widow or widower is entitled to inherit the pension at a rate of 50% of the pension payable originally to the contributor in addition to any entitlement in relation to the basic State pension.

Until 2000, nothing was payable to a widower and the rate payable to widows was 100%. The DSS (predecessor of the DWP) gave insufficient notice that the rate would come down for widows and it was therefore reduced in stages between October 2002 and October 2010. Meanwhile the rate of 50% has been payable to widowers.

From 2010, the rights available to surviving widows and widowers are extended to registered civil partners.

Key Facts

- On death before taking retirements and before age 75, the tax rules allow a lump sum to be paid that will usually be free of inheritance tax.
- The lump sum payable on death before retirement/75 will be measured against the lifetime allowance.
- Taking death benefits as income will never constitute a benefit crystallisation event.
- A defined benefit lump sum refers to a death benefit calculated by reference to a multiple of earnings, service or another factor linked to employment.
- An income may only be paid to a dependant on the member's death.
- A dependant is someone who is financially dependent or interdependent on the member.
- A spouse when the member's pension starts is assumed to be dependent.
- A child under the age of 23 is assumed to be dependent, as is a child who is dependent because of physical or mental impairment.
- Bereavement allowance is only payable for one year and is contributory.

QUESTIONS AND ANSWERS

Q1   From a tax perspective why must the trustees distribute the lump sum death benefit promptly?

A   There may be a charge to inheritance tax if the lump sum is not distributed within two years of death (or as soon as is otherwise practicable).

Q2   **Why will a member be asked to express a wish as to who should benefit rather than to nominate a beneficiary?**

A   The reason for this rather convoluted process is that if the member nominates, the nomination is binding, but the benefit forms part of his or her estate for inheritance tax purposes.

Q3   **When is a pension protection lump sum benefit payable on the death of a member?**

A   A pension protection lump sum death benefit is payable where the member has not reached age 75, the pension is in payment and the member has specified that it should be treated as a pension protection lump sum benefit.

Q4   **Who can be a dependant under a registered scheme?**

A   Broadly speaking anyone who is financially dependent or interdependent on the member. This automatically includes a spouse, civil partner or child under the age of 23. It may include a child who is dependent on grounds of physical or mental disability.

Q5   **For how long is widowed parent's allowance payable and how is it structured (in general terms)?**

A   The widowed parent's allowance is payable until the youngest child is 16 or 19 if at school. It comprises a basic allowance plus an earnings related addition.

Q6   **At what rate is the inherited second pension payable in 2012?**

A   50% of the member's entitlement.

CHAPTER 11

Divorce

Occupational and Personal Pension Schemes

The general law has developed the current approach to the breakdown of marriage and civil partnerships and the division of assets over the last 40 years. The main principle to emerge has been that "fault" has no part to play in the way assets are allocated. It has only been relatively recently (2000) that pension rights have been treated in a similar way to other assets.

In practice, very few settlements are determined by the court, although the court is required to agree the arrangements for the division of assets and the custody and care of children. In respect of property, the court will usually "rubber stamp" an agreement made by the parties by granting a "consent order".

Pensions present a special type of problem in this context. They can only provide benefits in a relatively narrow form in order to benefit from tax privileges and this condition continues to apply in the event of a divorce settlement. Part of the condition is that benefits can only be taken from normal minimum pension age (eg 55) and then only in the form of income or perhaps income and lump sum.

There has originally been a problem caused by the prohibition on assigning pension rights, but this was effectively overridden by the pension legislation.

There are now three main options for dealing with pension rights on divorce or break-up of a civil partnership.
1. The value of pension rights may simply be taken into account in the settlement ("offsetting"). So, to take a crude example, one party may

keep the house while the other retains the pension rights (this is a fairly unsatisfactory example because the assets are so fundamentally different).

2. Part of the pension benefit may be earmarked and divided when the member takes benefits at or beyond normal minimum pension age ("pension splitting"). This option is now rarely used because it has been overtaken by the sharing option. It was unsatisfactory because it did not allow for a "clean break". The member continued to be liable for tax on the whole pension and the earmarked pension came to an end when the member died or the claimant remarried or registered a new civil partnership.

3. The newest option is known as "pension sharing". It allows a clean break by reallocating a proportion of pension rights to the claimant. The reallocated amount may be retained by the original occupational scheme or may be transferred to another arrangement by the claimant or within four months of the order, the rights may be transferred by the trustees without consent to another arrangement (buy-out plan). If the rights are retained by the occupational scheme, the claimant becomes a member (pension credit member) with similar rights to other members.

If the share is to be applied to a personal pension plan, the claimant will be required to reallocate the share to a new plan in his or her own name.

The pension share may be a proportion of any amount between 0% and 100%. The share is the subject of negotiation between the parties and the claimant has certain rights of disclosure. The starting point is that the cash equivalent transfer value is divided equally and the case is made by each side for departing from that split. In coming to an agreement, the parties are likely to secure the services of an actuary as well as a solicitor.

Key Facts

- Following a divorce, the member's pension may be subject to offsetting, splitting or sharing.
- In calculating a pension share, the starting point is the cash equivalent transfer value.
- The share awarded may be between 0% and 100%.
- The share is usually agreed between the parties but must be endorsed by the court.

CHAPTER 12

Glossary

Accrual
The build-up of pension entitlement, eg $\frac{1}{60}$th of final salary for each year of service. It can also refer to an increase in money purchase funds.

Actuary
A practitioner who assesses investment and mortality risk in order to value and cost defined benefit schemes.

Added years
A facility to add years of accrual in return for an additional personal contribution. The member might buy one year to increase the pension by, say, $\frac{1}{60}$th.

Additional voluntary contributions (AVC)
Voluntary personal contributions to an occupational scheme.

Annual allowance
An annual personal allowance beyond which aggregate input from employer and member is taxed.

Annual limit
An annual personal allowance in respect of personal contributions, beyond which no tax relief is available.

Annuity
Literally, an income payable at least annually. Now refers to a contract with a life assurance company to pay an income in at least annual instalments. A *compulsory purchase annuity* is available for purchase by pension funds and a *purchase life annuity* is available for money from other sources (including the pension lump sum).

Annuities may offer a guaranteed income or a variable income. They may offer joint-life options and varying rates of increase.

Automatic enrolment   A requirement from 2012 for employers to enrol employees in a qualifying scheme.

Authorised payments   Payments from a registered pension scheme that do not incur additional rates of tax.

Balance of cost   The contribution required of the employer to ensure that a defined benefit scheme is properly funded.

Beneficiary   An individual who is regarded by legislation and the scheme as being financially dependent or interdependent on the member (and therefore entitled to dependant's benefits).

Benefit crystallisation event (BCE)   A transaction that requires payments to be measured against the lifetime allowance. This could include the payment of pension or pension commencement lump sum.

Bulk transfer   Transfer of more than one member as part of one transaction, for example on the takeover of a company and its scheme.

Buy-out policy   An annuity that allows the trustees to buy-out (transfer) their liability to an insurance company.

Career average scheme   A defined benefit scheme that calculates benefits by reference to salary averaged over the period of membership rather than the last year or few years.

Cash balance scheme   A scheme to which the employer pays lump sums without reference to pay.

Code of Practice   A statement of recommended practice published by the Pensions Regulator. It is not law, but may be influential in court.

Contract   A legally enforceable agreement between two parties.

Contract out	A facility to pay or redirect part of the National Insurance contribution in order to provide an alternative to SERPS/S2P through a private arrangement.
Contributions	Input from employer and/or member and /or HMRC to a pension scheme.
Covenant	A promise (eg to provide a certain benefit).
CPI (Consumer Prices Index)	A measure of inflation that excludes housing costs and is the preferred measure of the Government.
Defined benefit	The basis of funding a type of pension scheme where the benefit is prescribed by a formula and the contributor has to meet the cost.
Dependant	An individual who is financially dependent or interdependent on the member. This will automatically include a child (including adopted child) under the age of 23 and a spouse at date of death. It may also include a child who is over 22, but dependent because of physical or mental impairment. It is otherwise for the scheme administrator to determine dependence.
Direct payment scheme	A scheme whose contributions are collected and paid on behalf of members by the employer.
Department for Work and Pensions (DWP)	The Government department responsible for member protection legislation, the State pension scheme and contracting-out rules.
Enhanced annuity	An annuity whose rate is increased to reflect shorter life expectancy.
Enhanced protection	A means of protecting benefits from the lifetime allowance charge where the value of those funds was already close to or exceeded the lifetime allowance in 2006. Protection is subject to conditions including a restriction on further accrual.

Final salary scheme	A defined benefit scheme that bases benefits on salary in the last year of service or more often salary averaged over the last three years of service.
Financial Assistance Scheme	A compensation scheme funded from taxation and scheme assets of failed schemes that is available where employers have failed after 1997 and left an underfunded scheme which does not qualify for help from the Pension Protection Fund (PPF). The PPF became available from 2005.
Funded scheme	A scheme whose benefits are provided by a fund which is accumulated, invested and managed.
Guaranteed minimum pension (GMP)	A minimum level of pension required of a defined benefit scheme that was contracted-out before 6 April 1997. It roughly equalled SERPS given up.
Guaranteed payment period	A period of up to 10 years for which an annuity or pension may be paid regardless of the survival of the annuitant or member.
HM Revenue & Customs (HMRC)	A division of HM Treasury responsible for the collection of taxes and supervision of pension tax (and tax relief) rules.
Hybrid schemes	A scheme that combined defined benefit and money purchase benefits.
Ill-health retirement (involuntary retirement)	The facility to retire and take benefits earlier than normal minimum pension age because the member is permanently unable to carry on working in his or her normal job.
Inheritance tax (IHT)	A tax payable when property changes hands (especially on death).
Investment regulated	An investment-regulated pension scheme in the case of a personal pension scheme is one where the member or somebody connected with the member (eg a relative or business co-owner) is

114

able to direct, influence or advise on the manner of the investment by an arrangement. This would typically be a self-invested personal pension (SIPP).

In the case of an occupational scheme, the definition is met if there are 50 or fewer members and at least one of the members or somebody connected with him or her can direct, influence or advise on the manner of the investment. This would typically be a small self-administered scheme (SSAS).

Investment risk — The risk that an investment may go down as well as up.

Last option date — The deadline for exercising a right to transfer benefits from an occupational scheme.

LPI (limited price indexation) — A requirement for pensions to increase. The required rate is in line with the Retail Prices Index or Consumer Prices Index subject to a cap of either 5% or 2.5%.

Maxwell — A newspaper proprietor who stole money from the employer pension fund, thereby highlighting how weak the controls and governance of defined benefit schemes were. The result was the **Pensions Act 1995**.

Means testing — A process of assessing personal income and capital to determine if some State benefits are available to an individual.

Member — An individual who qualifies for benefits under a pension scheme either because he or she has contributed or because an employer has contributed for him or her.

Money purchase — A scheme funding basis where the contribution is defined but the benefit is subject to a number of factors such as investment returns, interest rates, mortality and administrative costs.

NEST (National Employment Savings Trust)	A low cost and heavily regulated pension scheme to be launched in 2011/12.
Net contributions	Contributions to which basic rate tax is added and invested by HMRC.
Net pay arrangement	A means of giving tax relief on personal contributions. The pension contribution is deducted from pay before tax is applied (but after National Insurance).
Normal pension age	The lowest age at which a member can retire and take benefits without having to seek the permission of the trustees and without actuarial reduction.
Normal retirement age/date	Little more than a target date for funding, but usually the same as normal pension age.
Normal minimum pension age	A minimum pension age from which pension benefits may be taken from a registered pension scheme without incurring unauthorised payment charges.
Notifiable events	Significant events that may affect the employer covenant and which must be notified to the Pensions Regulator (listed in a Code of Practice).
Occupational (pension) scheme	A scheme established by a sponsoring employer which determines its constitution.
Pension commencement lump sum	A lump sum payable at the same time as a member becomes entitled to a retirement pension. It is an authorised lump sum and is tax-free.
Pension credit	The share of a pension benefit/rights awarded to a claimant on dissolution of marriage.
Pension Protection Fund	A "safety net" for schemes that are underfunded when the employer goes into liquidation. The PPF ensures that a minimum level of benefit is available to members and dependants.

Pension sharing   The division of pension rights on dissolution of marriage.

Personal (pension) scheme   A scheme offered by a provider such as a life assurance company which individuals are invited to join and to which an employer may contribute.

Preservation   Rules that require the value of pension rights already accrued to be maintained.

Primary protection   A means of protecting funds that were already large on 5 April 2006 from the lifetime allowance.

Public sector/service scheme   A scheme established by statute to provide benefits for employees in the public sector and funded from public finances.

Reference scheme   A model scheme whose benefits must be reflected by a defined benefit scheme that has contracted-out since 6 April 1997.

Registered pension scheme   A scheme that is registered with HMRC for tax purposes.

Retail Prices Index   A measure of consumer prices that is used as a measure of increases in State pensions and private pensions.

Retirement annuity contract   A deferred annuity that was the forerunner of personal pensions until 1987.

Retirement benefits   Income and lump sum benefits available between the ages of 55 and 75.

Salary sacrifice   The facility to give up entitlement to pay in order that the employer will pay a (higher) pension contribution. This is not the same as a personal contribution which is paid after entitlement and National Insurance.

SERPS   The State earnings-related pension scheme made available to employees between 1978 and 2002.

S2P	A variation on SERPS allowing different accrual for different earnings bands. It followed SERPS in 2002.
Self-invested personal pension (SIPP)	A personal pension that is able to invest in assets as directed by the member.
Small self-administered scheme	An occupational scheme that is able to invest in assets as directed by the member and comprising 12 or fewer members.
Special annual allowance	An allowance beyond which the member was to pay tax on contributions if a high income individual. It was due to be implemented in 2011, but was abandoned. In the meantime, higher income individuals were subject to "anti-forestalling" measures pending an adjustment to the annual allowance rules from 6 April 2011.
State pension	A pension provided by the State. It is contributory (qualification based on national insurance record) and funded from current taxation and National Insurance.
State pension credit	A means-tested benefit available to supplement low retirement income.
Statement of investment principles	A statutory requirement of defined benefit schemes that sets the principles the trustees should observe when considering investment strategy and lays out the means of monitoring performance.
Statement of funding principles	The trustees are required to prepare and maintain a statement of funding principles to ensure that the statutory funding objective is met. The written statement includes: • funding objectives and the trustees' policy for ensuring that the objective is met • implications of funding on scheme investment policy

- methods and assumptions to be used in calculating technical provisions; and
- a period over which failure to meet the statutory funding objective will be rectified.

Statutory funding objective The statutory funding objective is scheme specific and places an obligation on trustees to agree a strategy for meeting pension commitments with the sponsoring employer.

Technical provisions Scheme liabilities.

The Pensions Advisory Service A charity established by statute to provide technical support and advice.

The Pensions Ombudsman An office for dealing with disputes between members and connected parties and pension schemes.

The Pensions Regulator A regulatory body established by law to promote work-based pension schemes and to supervise their good administration.

Transitional protection Protection given to pension schemes that had accrued benefits prior to 6 April 2006 against the lifetime allowance and unauthorised payment charges that might otherwise apply. Protection includes enhanced and primary protection, pension commencement lump sum protection and protection of low pension ages.

Trustee An individual or company responsible for collecting contributions, managing investments and paying benefits within the rules of the pension scheme. The trustee differs from an administrator in that he or she is the legal owner of assets that will be used to give effect to pension rights.

Unsecured pension An option to draw a variable retirement income directly from a money purchase fund rather than to purchase an annuity or take a scheme pension. The term has been replaced by "drawdown pension" from 6 April 2011.

GLOSSARY

Work-based scheme An occupational or personal pension scheme for which an employer operates a direct payment arrangement (ie pays contributions and operates a facility to collect member contributions through pay and pass them to the scheme). The term has been replaced by'drawdown pension' from 6 April 2011.

Index

G

H

I

J

L

M